The Story of Ethel and Julius Rosenberg

A Courtroom and Prison Drama Set in the 1950's in New York City.

Nina Serrano
Paul Richards
Judith Binder

ESTUARY PRESS

D1082498

The Story of Ethel and Julius Rosenberg

Cover art and title page art by Beryl Landau

Cover and book design by Paul Richards

Table of Contents

How The Story of Ethel and Julius Rosenberg Came to Be

By Nina Serrano

The *The Story of Ethel and Julius Rosenberg* is a play I co-authored in 1976. My journey to creating the script began years before in 1953, when Ethel and Julius Rosenberg were executed at Sing Sing Prison in Ossining, NY. I was an 18 year old theatre student in New York City where I witnessed one of the most controversial trials in US history convicting the Rosenbergs of conspiracy to commit espionage for handing over the so called secrets of the atom bomb to the Soviet Union. It was the crowning moment of the infamous McCarthy anti-communist era.

Nina Serrano as Ethel, Joseph Ingala as Judge, and John Parkinson as Julius in 1976 production photo. 1975, San Francisco, CA.

Cold War hysteria that followed the World War II went into high gear when the Soviet Union exploded their first atom bomb in 1949. Fake science of that era then created the myth of "atom bomb secrets" to use in the witch hunt to turn people against the Soviet Union, our former ally in the war against German and Japanese fascism. The hunt for communist spies provided the anti-communist crusade with more opportunity to escalate its attacks on dissenters at home. Fear of atomic war, like the fear of terrorism today since 9/11, was used successfully to frighten and manipulate the population into silence. Bomb shelters were built into schools, duck and cover drills in anticipation of atomic bomb attack went on across the country. Mass hysteria came to a head in the indictment and prosecution of a young Jewish couple for allegedly giving the atom bomb secrets to the USSR.

1976 cast of The Story of Ethel and Julius Rosenberg. L to R: Paul Richards, Robert Galitzen, Nina Serrano, John Parkinson and Judith Binder. Production Photo .

But not everyone was silenced. The international movement for justice for the Rosenbergs swept many countries of the world with massive protests. In the New York City Broadway arts community where I was active, a few leading figures spoke out against the kangaroo court. My drama teacher, actor, director, writer Howard da Silva was one, along with other blacklisted professional New York actors like Morris Carnovsky and Phoebe Brand, founders of the historic Group Theater in New York. They staged readings of the Rosenbergs' letters and went on tour in an effort to save them. As the baby sitter for the da Silva's children, I heard many rehearsals in their living room. I remember the tremendous sadness I felt around the Rosenberg's tragic deaths in the electric chair after an unjust trial. The mainstream US press reviled them in their sensationalized covered of the tragic events.

Years later, as an adult and mother of two, I made frequent visits to revolutionary Cuban where I was surprised to find a monument to the Rosenbergs on a major Havana thoroughfare. Over the intervening years the Rosenberg's sons were adopted as children by the song writer Abel Meeropol, author of the iconic song "Strange Fruit" made popular by Billie Holiday. They took the Meeropol name and became professors. They continued to protest their parent's unjust murder and founded the Rosenberg Fund for Children to help other children of political dissenters suffering persecution here in the United States. The Rosenberg's famous international cause touched Cuban hearts and today the Rosenberg monument appears in tourist literature.

In 1975, my friend, film maker Estela Bravo invited me to join her in a new project, The Rosenberg Brigade. I had worked with Estela earlier in those pre-computer days assisting on a project to archive American folk and protest music at Casa de las Americas, the leading cultural institution in Cuba. The Rosenberg Brigade was a Cuban theatrical group that toured rural boarding schools and other outposts in the countryside to present live readings of the letters of Ethel and Julius Rosenberg in Spanish with slides of the Rosenbergs and press clippings. The letters of Ethel were read by the famous exiled Chilean TV star Mirella LaTorre. The performances were always well received, the audiences deeply moved by this family drama with the love letters between the couple and their tragic deaths, leaving behind two small children.

Upon my return to California in 1976, Paul Richards contacted me with a proposal to write a multi-media piece about Ethel and Julius Rosenberg. Paul had gone to graduate school with the Rosenberg's son, Michael Meeropol, in Madison Wisconsin and was an Assistant Professor of History at the time we met. I brought in my experienced artistic team, my brother Philip Serrano for music, Judith Binder for writing and direction, and Beryl Landau for Graphics. Paul dived right into the one thousand page trial transcript and other sources and came up with some juicy quotes on file cards. We wrote a full blown drama. In the meantime, Paul and I fell in love and 12 years later, married.

The play "The Story of Ethel and Julius Rosenberg" premiered at La Peña Cultural Center, Berkeley in 1976 and then toured Bay Area Colleges and finally was performed on KPFA-Radio and KQED-TV. Philip Serrano wrote a theme song for the play. In our original production, I played Ethel and Paul played her villainous brother David Greenglass. Judith Binder directed and played the Narrator.

Judith Binder and Nina Serrano during the writing of the play. 1975, San Francisco, CA.. Photo by Paul Richards

Leaflet announcing The Story of Ethel and Julius Rosenberg, 1976. Leaflet by Beryl Landau with Picasso drawings of Ethel and Julius.

The Story of Ethel and Julius Rosenberg (1976)

A Courtroom and Prison Drama Set in the 1950's in New York City.

CHARACTERS

Ethel Rosenberg

Julius Rosenberg

The Defense

The Prosecution

Judge Irving Kaufman

David Greenglass

Narrator

Bob Consodine

Note: The character of the DEFENSE is the composite dialogues of Alexander and Emmanuel Bloch. The PROSECUTION is the composite of Roy Cohn and Irving Saypol.

The play is performed without an intermission.

THE SETTING

A judge's bench is upstage center. There is one courtroom chair stage right of the judge's bench and two chairs stage left of the Judge's bench. Two jail cots are downstage, one stage right and one stage left. The set remains the same throughout the play.

THEME MUSIC

Theme Music composed by Philip Serrano. (To hear the song, go to YouTube https://youtu.be/IdKJ8HOFY9c)

COSTUMES

Costumes: All the characters are dressed in clothes of the late 1940's and early fifties except the narrator who is in contemporary clothes.

SLIDE SHOW

In the original production, there were 80 slides.

The Narrator operated the slide machine to illustrate the narration. Photos were found in newspapers and magazines from the Rosenberg's arrest in June 1950 to their execution in June, 1953. Highly recommended sources of photographs are:

We Are Your Sons by Michael and Robert Meeropol, Houghton-Mifflin, 1975, and University of Illinois Press, Subsequent Edition, 1986.

Invitation to An Inquest by Walter and Miriam Schnier, Pantheon Books, 1983.

The Unquiet Death of Ethel and Julius Rosenberg, by Alvin H. Goldstein, Lawrence Hill Books, 1975.

LIGHTS

The lights indicate the location of the action, e.g. on courtroom, jail cots, etc.

THE PLAY

A pool of light fades up center stage on Ethel and Julius. They are alone dancing a foxtrot to the theme music as if it were from a radio in their living room. Within a minute, their dance is interrupted by the voice and presence of the defense who enters stage left and comes up to the edge of the pool of light, but remains in the darkness.

DEFENSE: What is your full name?

The couple are interrupted in their dance. They open up with one arm still around the other. JULIUS responds to the questions. MUSIC cuts off.

JULIUS: Julius Rosenberg.

DEFENSE: And how old are you?

JULIUS: 33.

DEFENSE: Where were you born?

JULIUS: I was born in New York City.

DEFENSE: And were you educated here in New York City?

JULIUS: Yes I was. At the same time that I attended Public school I attended Hebrew School. I entered the School of Technology of the College of the City of New York in June 1934 and I attained my degree of a Bachelor of Electrical engineering in February of 1939.

DEFENSE: To whom are you married?

JULIUS: I am married to Ethel Rosenberg.

DEFENSE: Now, is she the lady who was sitting next to you at the counsel table and is sitting right now here?

JULIUS: Yes, Sir.

He turns to ETHEL, takes her in his arms and they continue to dance. Music fades in. The DEFENSE walks in the darkness, circling around in the darkness upstage behind Ethel. His question again interrupts the dance. This time the couple separate lightly.

DEFENSE (to Ethel) Are you married?

ETHEL: Yes

DEFENSE: To whom?

ETHEL: Julius Rosenberg.

DEFENSE: The other defendant in this case?

ETHEL: That is right.

DEFENSE: And you are a defendant in this case?

ETHEL: Yes, I am.

DEFENSE: What was your maiden name?

ETHEL: Ethel Greenglass.

DEFENSE: How many brothers and sisters have you?

ETHEL: I have three brothers. . . . David, Bernard and Sam.

DEFENSE: How many children have you?

ETHEL: I have two children. . . . Michael was eight March tenth and Robert will be four, May eleventh.

She turns to JULIUS and goes into his arms. They continue dancing to the theme music which has faded up. They dip and turn playfully, enjoying the intimacy as if dancing in their own living room.

Dim LIGHT fades up on the NARRATOR AS ETHEL AND JULIUS continue dancing.

NARRATOR: This is the story of Ethel and Julius Rosenberg. The actors will tell it in the Rosenberg's own words and the words of other historical figures as preserved in their letters, the court record and other documents of the time.

NARRATOR opens the book on the music stand in front of her. As the music and lights on the Rosenbergs fade out, they turn to face the screen behind them.

The NARRATOR reads from the book as SLIDES on the screen illustrate the talk.

NARRATOR: The story begins in 1945. The United States atomic bombs explode on the cities of Nagasaki and Hiroshima. The World War II big three alliance between the U. S., Britain and Russia breaks up into the cold war confrontation. Anti-communism and nuclear monopoly dominates U.S. foreign policy. Seven Chicago scientists predict in 1945 that the Soviet Union would develop an atomic bomb in a few years. They believe that the Soviets have both the industrial capacity and the scientific technology to produce the bomb.

In June of 1947, the Military Industrial complex, through the National Association of Manufacturers (to which the multi-national corporations belong) write and lobby for the Taft Hartley act. The Taft Hartley act puts legal limitations on the worker' s rights to organize and makes it illegal for Communists to hold union office. Communists and suspected Communists are purged.

*LIGHTS out on NARRATOR and SCREEN. THEME MUSIC
fades up and Ethel and Julius continue dancing. The
THEME MUSIC ends and the MUSIC of UNION MAID comes
up. They continue dancing to the livelier music and sing
along with it. They waltz and sing as if singing along to the
music on the radio.*

ETHEL AND JULIUS: (sing)

> THERE ONCE WAS A UNION MAID

> WHO NEVER WAS AFRAID

> OF GOONS AND GINKS AND COMPANY FINKS

> AND THE DEPUTY SHERIFFS WHO MADE THE RAIDS

> SHE WENT TO THE UNION HALL

> WHEN A MEETING IT WAS CALLED

> AND WHEN THE LEGION BOYS CAME ROUND

> SHE ALWAYS STOOD HER GROUND.

> OH, YOU CAN'T SCARE ME I'M STICKING TO THE UNION

> I'M STICKING TO THE UNION

> I'M STICKING TO THE UNION

> OH, YOU CAN'T SCARE ME, I'M STICKING TO THE UNION

> I'M STICKING TO THE UNION TILL THE DAY I DIE

*They twirl around, laughing. Julius spins Ethel out under his
arm. He ends up in front of the two chairs stage left of the
Judge's bench. She is stage right of the bench. DEFENSE
Enters in the darkness behind them.*

DEFENSE: What union did you belong to?

The dance is interrupted. Music stops.

JULIUS: The Federation of Architects and Engineers.

DEFENSE: And what did you do during most of the years in that union in terms of activity?

JULIUS: Well, for a period of time I was chairman of the Federal Civil Service committee of that union.

DEFENSE: And in connection with that activity, did you help members of that union with respect to keeping their positions?

JULIUS: That is correct.

DEFENSE: And did you handle grievance cases?

JULIUS: Yes.

DEFENSE: For that union?

JULIUS: Yes.

As ETHEL and JULIUS turn toward each other, the PROSECUTOR and JUDGE enter in the darkness behind them. the JUDGE sits on his bench. The prosecutor stands opposite Bloch outside the pool of light. ETHEL and JULIUS move toward each other to continue their dance. They are interrupted by the PROSECUTOR.

PROSECUTOR: Is it not a fact that you were removed from government service because you were a member of the Communist party?

DEFENSE: If the court please... if the prosecutor wants a concession, I will concede right now that this witness was removed from Government service upon charges that he was a member of the Communist Party.

PROSECUTOR: Were you a member of the Communist Party?

JULIUS: I refuse to answer on the ground that it might incriminate me.

PROSECUTOR exits.

DEFENSE: (to ETHEL) What union did you belong to?

ETHEL: I was a member of the ladies auxiliary of the Federation of Architects and Engineers which was my husband's union and I did a lot of typing for them, and when I worked at National packing I was a member of a shipping clerks union. When I worked at Bell Textile Company, I was' a member of Local 65 of the United Wholesale and Retail.

DEFENSE: Were you active in the union?

ETHEL: Yes, I was.

POOL OF LIGHT on ETHEL and JULIUS fades out as light fades up on Narrator. ETHEL and JULIUS turn to face screen behind them. SLIDES on screen illustrate Narration.

NARRATOR: In Washington, D.C., the military are given control of atomic energy. The scientists are silenced under a policy of secrecy. The U.S. military declares that the key to our nation's strength and survival is nuclear monopoly. The political climate changes to widespread secrecy, security clearance and loyalty oaths. In 1949, the Soviets explode the atom bomb, as scientists had predicted. The cold warriors insist that the Soviets are only able to do it because the United States secrets have been stolen. J. Edgar Hoover launches a highly publicized search for Soviet espionage agents. The FBI search becomes an attack on all American dissidents.

LIGHT out on NARRATOR and SCREEN. LIGHT up on JULIUS AND ETHEL. They open their arms to each other and start to come together to continue their dance. They are interrupted before they reach each other.

DEFENSE: Now did there come a time when you went into business?

JULIUS: In the spring of 1946 we entered into a new partnership.

DEFENSE: And who were the members of the firm?

JULIUS: My brothers-in-law, Bernard Greenglass and David Greenglass, a neighbor, Isidore Goldstein ... and myself.

DEFENSE: And what was the business?

JULIUS: It was a machine shop.

DEFENSE: (to ETHEL) Now, your brother, David Greenglass, was the youngest in the family...and you were 6 years older than he was, and what was the relationship between you throughout the period of your living together in the same household, until you married and after you married?

ETHEL: Well, he was my baby brother.

DEFENSE: Did you treat him as such?

ETHEL: Yes, that is exactly how I treated him.

DEFENSE: Did you love him?

ETHEL: Yes, I loved him very much.

LIGHT out on ETHEL AND JULIUS. LIGHT up on NARRATOR and SLIDES. ETHEL AND JULIUS turn to face the screen.

NARRATOR: In 1950, Ethel and Julius Rosenberg live with their two sons, Michael and Robbie in lower income housing in New York City. Ethel grew up in a poor family in New York, one of four children including her brother, David Greenglass. Julius, one of five children, also grew up in New York. He went to City College where he was a politically active left winger like so many of his generation in the midst of the great depression. During that time he met and married Ethel Greenglass. In 1950, Julius is an engineer working in a small machine shop in an unhappy partnership with his brother-in-law, David Greenglass. In February, 1950, during the government's search for atomic spies, David Greenglass is questioned about the theft of uranium during World War II from the Los Alamos atom bomb project where he had worked as a machinist. On June fifteenth, he is arrested. David is questioned again, this time about atomic espionage.

LIGHT out on NARRATOR and SLIDES. LIGHT up on ETHEL and JULIUS. They turn front and move toward each other to continue dancing. They are interrupted before they can touch by a voice from the darkness.

DEFENSE: (to JULIUS) In June, 1950, were you interrogated by the FBI?

JULIUS: Yes. Once.

DEFENSE: When?

JULIUS: The morning after the FBI took David Greenglass in custody. They came to my house. There were three men. They said, "We are from the FBI. We would like to talk to you." I asked my wife, "Do you think I ought to talk to these gentlemen?" She said, "You know, if Davey is in some sort of trouble, if you can help my brother, talk to them; maybe you can be of some assistance to them." I said, "I will talk to you gentlemen." and I finished dressing the children; my wife made some breakfast; I took my shave; and they looked around the apartment and said, "We can't talk here. Would you like to come down to our office and have a cup of coffee?" And I went with the gentlemen of the FBI about 9 o'clock I believe.

DEFENSE: (crosses downstage left, still outside the pool of light) Now tell us what was said by the FBI agents to you and what you said to them, and how long you stayed there.

JULIUS: They started asking questions about what I knew about David Greenglass. First they tried to get my background, what relations I had with him. I gave them my school background, work background and I told them whatever I knew about David Greenglass's education and his work background. . . . At one point in the discussion, I would say it was about two hours after I was there, they said to me, "Do you know that your brother-in-law said you told him to supply information for Russia?"

So I says, "That couldn't be true...where is David Greenglass?" I didn't know where he was because I knew he was taken into custody. They wouldn't tell me. I said, "Will you bring him here and let him tell me that to my face?" And they said, "What if we bring him here, what will you do?" "I will call him a liar to his face because that is not so." And I said, "Look gentlemen, at first you asked me to come down and get some information concerning David Greenglass. Now you are trying to implicate me in something. I would like to see a lawyer."

JUDGE: And you didn't say anything about David's request for money in May or June of 1950, nor did you tell them the story as I understand it, of David's anticipated thefts from the Army which were related to you by Ruth Greenglass in February, 1945?

JULIUS: (crosses to the judge's bench) No, I didn't tell them, your honor. The way I was brought up, I don't inform on my wife's brother, and whatever he did, I didn't know about and that is for him to decide, for him to answer.

DEFENSE: (to ETHEL) Did you talk to your sister-in-law, Ruth, after the arrest of your brother?

ETHEL: At my mother's house . . . I says, "Look Ruth, I would like to know something: Are you and Davey really mixed up in this horrible mess?" . . . and she said, "What are you a asking such silly questions for? He is not guilty and of course I am not guilty and we have hired a lawyer and we are going to fight this case because we are not guilty. Did you think we were?" And I said, "Look, I really did not know what to think any more. There have been reports in the newspapers about confessions and much as I believed, always believed in Davey, I had to hear it from your own lips. And she said, "Well now you have heard it and it is the truth. Neither as us is guilty."

DEFENSE: That is the last talk you had with her?

ETHEL: That is right.

DEFENSE AND JUDGE exit. Lights go out on ETHEL and JULIUS as they turn to face the screen. The SLIDES come on while the LIGHT fades up dim on the NARRATOR who continues reading.

NARRATOR: David and Ruth Greenglass are charged with conspiracy to commit atomic espionage. The conspiracy law allows the government to prosecute someone without having to prove anything but intention to act, rather than the act itself. David and his wife Ruth agree to cooperate with government prosecutors. Their word becomes enough to convict those they accuse of being accomplices. On June 25, 1950, ten days after David's arrest, the Korean war breaks out and U.S. troops go into combat against Communism in Asia. Patriotism and anti-Communism reach fever pitch. David Greenglass names his brother-in-law as a conspirator. Julius Rosenberg is arrested on July 17, 1950.

JULIUS crosses to his cell downstage left as light goes out on SLIDES.

NARRATOR: The FBI's report of Julius Rosenberg's arrest reads: "Ethel, his wife, made a typical communist remonstrance demanding a warrant and the right to call an attorney. She was told to keep quiet and get in the other room with the children which she did." Julius is housed in Federal Prison in New York City.

LIGHT out on NARRATOR. LIGHT up full on JULIUS in his cell.

JULIUS: July 24, 1950. Dearest wife and two boys, I am allowed to send you three letters a week. This afternoon before supper I had a talk with the visiting Rabbi. He's a nice guy and if the front office will permit him, he will call Mom and tell her I'm alright. I hear your brother David was shipped off to the tombs.

THEME MUSIC fades in softly. ETHEL stands in a pool of light.

ETHEL: July 25, 1950. Dearest Julie. This will have to be brief as it is now close to 1:00 AM and my eyes ache for lack of sleep. Just got through hanging the clothes as Mike didn't get off to sleep until 11:30. Have an awful lot scheduled before I see you again. The accountant is coming in Thursday. Received a number of bills, two of which are telephone bills. How long can I wait to pay bills? Love you darling" miss you and can't wait until Sunday, when I'll be able to visit you--in prison. I can't believe it yet.

ETHEL exits right. Theme music fades out.

Lights go up on NARRATOR and SLIDES.

NARRATOR: David Greenglass is housed in the Tombs prison with Harry Gold who faces a thirty year sentence in another case for allegedly being a spy.

Gold, an unstable individual who lived in a world of fantasy, came forward of his own accord claiming to be the American courier for Klaus Fuchs who had confessed to passing information to Soviet agents while he worked in Los Alamos during World War II. Fuchs, a German born British scientist, described the man he passed material to as older and taller than Gold and refused to identify Gold a number of times. The U.S. Government to this day refuses to make public Fuchs actual written confession. Greenglass and Gold, together in the Tombs for nine months were friendly witnesses for the government and had many discussions with each other, the FBI and the prosecutors. Two months' after his arrest, David Greenglass, who has already implicated Julius, states that his sister, Ethel is not involved.

LIGHT out on slide and NARRATOR. LIGHT up on chair stage right of judge's bench. GREENGLASS enters and sits in the chair, the PROSECUTOR enters and stands above GREENGLASS as the NARRATOR continues speaking.

NARRATOR: In August, 1950, the District Attorney questions David before the Grand Jury that later indicted Ethel and Julius.

PROSECUTOR: Was Ethel present in any of these occasions in 1945?

DAVID: Never.

PROSECUTOR: Did Ethel ever talk to you about it?

DAVID: Never spoke about it to me, and that's a fact. Aside from trying to protect my sister, believe me, that's a fact.

PROSECUTOR and GREENGLASS exit as LIGHTS go out on stage and up on NARRATOR and slides.

NARRATOR: These are times of hysteria in the United States. Suspicion becomes the mark of the times. The word of brother used against sister is sufficient to convict and execute. The Cold War makes its deepest penetration of American society, inside an American family. David's story is changed to implicate his sister. Ethel is arrested one month after her husband.

LIGHT out on Slides and NARRATOR. LIGHT up on ETHEL in her jail cell, She is in a prison dress, pacing and singing to give herself courage.

ETHEL: (sings)

DIE GEDUNKEN SIND FREI

MY THOUGHTS ALWAYS FREE

MY THOUGHTS GIVE ME PLEASURE

MY THOUGHTS WILL NOT CATER TO DUKE OR DICTATOR

AND FREE MEN WILL SING

MY THOUGHTS ALWAYS FREE

SO THROW ME IN JAIL

AND CLOSE THE DOOR ON ME

MY THOUGHTS THEY WILL BLOSSOM

LIKE FLOWERS IN SPRINGTIME

AND FREE MEN WILL SING

DIE GEDUNKEN SIND FREI

ETHEL: August 12, 1950. My dearest Darling Julie. By now you must know what has happened to me. . .. My heart cries aloud for you and the children and I must confess that my mind does leap ahead to the frightening possibilities for them. . . . Sweetheart, I talk with you every night before I fall asleep and cry because you can't hear me. And then I tell myself that you too must be choking with the same frustration and wondering if I can hear you. Darling, we mustn't lose each other or the children, mustn't loose our identities. I try to think of the good, fine life we have led all these years and I am agonized with my longing to go on leading it. . . . I love you, Ethel.

NARRATOR: After Ethel's arrest, the children go to the home of Ethel and David"s mother, Tessie Greenglass. A relative writes to Ethel: "Your ma reviles and rants about you and the situation you and Julie brought on her family and how much trouble the kids are and how bad they are and how bad you are, and why don't you do what Ruthie did so you too could be with your kids."

DEFENSE enters in darkness, LIGHT out on NARRATOR and up on ETHEL in her cell.

DEFENSE: Where are your children now?

ETHEL, They are at a temporary shelter in the Bronx.

DEFENSE: Have you seen them since you were arrested?

ETHEL: No, I have not.

DEFENSE exists. LIGHT out on ETHEL. LIGHT up on NARRATOR and Slides

NARRATOR: The anti-communist inquisition grows into a national obsession. Richard H. Nixon, a young Congressman from California, makes a name for himself as part of the prosecution of suspected communists in the State Department. Joseph McCarthy, Senator from Wisconsin, dominates television and newspaper headlines for months with his list of names of reds in the government. Two Presidents Harry S. Truman and Dwight D. Eisenhower, are swept along by the tide. Patriotism becomes the order of the day. "Stand up and be an American." It is implied that the model for Americanism is a the white Anglo-Saxon Protestant who supports business over labor, spending for guns over spending for people and, above all, someone who doesn't question our government's policies at home or abroad. People are convicted, condemned and jailed for their beliefs. The Fifth Amendment echoes in the courtrooms.

"I have a right to remain silent against self-incrimination." People are afraid, knowing that if they are suspect, admitting merely to knowing someone makes the other person suspect, too. Many people take the Fifth Amendment so they won't be forced to harm others. In Asia, China has a successful communist revolution. Civil War breaks out in Korea. Vietnamese led by Ho Chi Minh fight against French Colonialism. American intervention in Korea is a first step into a costlier even bloodier war in Indo-china. In October, 1950, in Latin America, Puerto Rican Nationalists demand independence from the U. S. In 1951, Puerto Rican nationalists attempt to assassinate President Harry

S. Truman, in Washington, D.C. In Africa, the black world protests. Independence struggles deepen and bring new independent African nations into being. Black Americans find crosses burning in their yards and are lynched by racist mobs. Americans are frightened into building bomb shelters. Air raid drills are rehearsed in the schools and children given identification tags in case of war the Communist Russians.

LIGHT out on NARRATOR and Slides. LIGHTS fade up dim on the courtroom. PROSECUTOR enters with flag and puts the pole in a stand. GREENGLASS enters and stands in front of his chair. DEFENSE enters and stands next to 2 empty chairs JUDGE enters, steps up on the bench and stands.

NARRATOR: In this environment, in March, 1951, eight months after their arrest, Ethel and Julius Rosenberg go on trial accused of conspiracy to commit espionage, for stealing the secrets of the atom bomb.

ETHEL and JULIUS rise from their jail cots. They take their coats from under the cots and put them on. ETHEL puts on her hat and picks up her purse as JULIUS puts on his tie and buttons his jacket. They step out into the space between their two cells and face each other. Their wrists are crossed together as if by handcuffs. ETHEL lifts her hands with wrists crossed, to JULIUS' face. He lifts his arms with wrists crossed, over her head and shoulders. They kiss. They come out of their embrace, turn to face the courtroom. Their wrists release as they walk side by side to their chairs. ETHEL is at the chair right. JULIUS is to her left. They turn to face front and stand.

NARRATOR: Judge Irving Kaufman presides.

JUDGE, the ROSENBERGS and GREENGLASS sit.

PROSECUTOR; Ladies and Gentlemen of the jury...the evidence will show that the loyalty of the Rosenbergs was not to this country, but that it was to Communism -- Communism in this country and Communism throughout the world.

DEFENSE: (Crosses to the JUDGE) If the court pleases. I object to these remarks . . . because Communism is not on trial here.

JUDGE: The charge here is espionage. It is not that the defendants are members of the Communist Party or that they had any interest in Communism. However, if the Government intends to establish that they did have an interest in Communism, for the purpose of establishing a motive for what they were doing I will, in due course, when that question arises, rule on that point. . . .

DEFENSE crosses and stands left of JULIUS

DEFENSE: Excuse me, I think I said to the jury that the charge was espionage. I want to correct that. The charge is conspiracy to commit espionage.

PROSECUTOR Stands behind GREENGLASS

PROSECUTOR: David Greenglass, have you entered a plea to that indictment...charging conspiracy to commit espionage?

GREENGLASS: I have

PROSECUTOR: What is that plea?

GREENGLASS: Guilty.

PROSECUTOR Crosses to the left of GREENGLASS.

PROSECUTOR: Your sister is the defendant, Mrs. Ethel Greenglass Rosenberg, is that correct?

GREENGLASS: That is true.

PROSECUTOR: And another defendant, Julius Rosenberg, is your brother-in-law?

GREENGLASS: That is true.

PROSECUTOR: Now did you have any discussion with Ethel and Julius concerning the relative merits of our form of government and that of the Soviet Union?

DAVID opens his mouth to speak. He is interrupted by Defense Attorney. DEFENSE crosses to JUDGE.

DEFENSE: Objected to as incompetent, irrelevant and immaterial, not pertinent to the issues raised in the indictment and the plea. This will obviously lead to matters which will make it difficult or almost impossible for the jury to confine themselves to the real issues in the case.

PROSECUTOR: (Crosses to JUDGE) Your Honor. Of course the views of the defendants on the relative merits of this country and the Soviet Union are extremely relevant when the charge is conspiracy to commit espionage, in that material would be transferred to the Soviet Union to be used to the advantage of the Soviet Union.

JUDGE: What you are trying to bring out from the witness is the fact that the defendants expressed some form of favoritism to Russia in their discussions?

PROSECUTOR: Exactly, Your honor.

JUDGE: I believe it is relevant. . . . Objection overruled.

DEFENSE crosses down left. PROSECUTOR turns to GREENGLASS.

PROSECUTOR: You may now answer.

GREENGLASS: I did have such discussions.

PROSECUTOR: Over what period of time, roughly?

JUDGE: Please speak up Mr. Greenglass.

GREENGLASS: From about 1935 to about 1946.

PROSECUTOR: Talking about Socialism over Capitalism, did they specifically talk about Socialism as it existed in the Soviet Union and Capitalism as it existed here?

GREENGLASS: They did.

Crosses to the right of GREENGLASS.

PROSECUTOR: Which did they like better? Did they tell you?

GREENGLASS: They preferred Socialism to Capitalism,

JUDGE: Which type of Socialism?

GREENGLASS: Russian Socialism?

PROSECUTOR Crosses to Julius.

PROSECUTOR:Did you do anything else besides talk in respect to your feeling . . . about the Russian position in the war?

JULIUS: I don't understand what you mean.

PROSECUTOR: Did you ever go out and collect any money for the joint Anti-Fascist Refugee Committee?

JULIUS: I don't recall collecting any money, but I recall contributing money.

PROSECUTOR: (holds up can) Do you remember when the agents arrested you and they took that out of your house?

JULIUS: That is correct.

PROSECUTOR: And the can reads on the label, "Save a Spanish Republican Child, Volveremos, We will return, joint Anti-Fascist Refugee Committee" and there is a notice on the back that the City of New York permits these cans to be used for solicitation. So that perhaps you did a little more them just contribute.

He turns, puts the can on the JUDGES bench and walks to GREENGLASS.

PROSECUTOR: Did you give to Rosenberg a description of the atom bomb itself?

GREENGLASS: I did.

PROSECUTOR: When did you give the first sketch? The first lens mold sketch?

GREENGLASS: That was in January, 1945.

PROSECUTOR: To whom did you give it?

33

GREENGLASS: I gave that to Julius Rosenberg.

PROSECUTOR crosses behind GREENGLASS.

DEFENSE: Mr. Rosenberg, did you ever receive a sketch of a cross section of the atom bomb from David Greenglass or Ruth Greenglass at anytime?

JULIUS: No I did not.

DEFENSE: You received a telephone call from Ruth in February, 1945.

JULIUS: That's right.

DEFENSE: And what did she say to you?

JULIUS: She would like to see me.

DEFENSE: Tell us what happened when you went over to see her.

JULIUS: Ruthie told me something to this effect: "Julius, I am terribly worried. David has an idea to make some money and take some things from the Army"; and I told her, "Warn David not to do anything foolish. He will only get himself in trouble."

DEFENSE: (crosses to ETHEL) Now, will you give us, as far as you can recollect the substance of what your husband told you and what you told him at the time?

ETHEL: Julius came home and he said that Ruth was kind of worried about some crazy notions that Dave had about making some money, about taking some things, and I said, "Well what did you tell her? Did you make sure to tell her to warn him about it, not to do it?" He said "Yes, that he had." And I said,

"Well all right, then I guess there is nothing to worry about."

PROSECUTOR: (crosses to the left of GREENGLASS) Now will you tell us just what happened, Mr. Greenglass, after you handed the sketch and the descriptive material concerning the atomic bomb to Rosenberg? What did he do, and what did the others there do?

DAVID: Well, he stepped into another room and he read it and he came out and he said "this is very good. We ought to have this typed immediately." And my wife said, "We will probably have to correct the grammar involved," because I was more interested in writing down the technical phrases of it than in correcting the grammar. So they. . . had a bridge table and they brought it into the living room, plus a typewriter.

PROSECUTOR crosses up center and turns to ETHEL.

PROSECUTOR: Who did the typing, Mr. Greenglass?

JUDGE: Now, Mr. Greenglass, would you please remember to speak up.

DAVID: Ethel did the typing and Ruth and Julius and Ethel did the correction of the grammar.

DEFENSE: (to JULIUS) Did you ever receive such a report or description in writing?

JULIUS: I did not receive any such description or report.

DEFENSE: (to ETHEL) Did you ever type any such information?

ETHEL: No, I never did.

35

DEFENSE: Or copy any writing that had been made by your brother in which information concerning the atomic bomb was alluded to?

ETHEL: I never did.

DEFENSE: (crosses to left of JULIUS) Now did you see Dave that month, May, 1950?

JULIUS: Yes, I did. . . . About the middle of May . . . David came to my shop one morning and he said, "Come on outside, I want to talk to you."

DEFENSE: (crosses behind JULIUS and ETHEL) Tell us about the conversation you had.

JULIUS, Dave said to me, "Julie, you got to get me $2000. I need it at once." I said, "Look, Dave, I just don't have the money. What do you need it for?" He said, "I need the money. Don't ask me questions." I recall at the time in my mind the incident--I thought maybe it had something to do with a conversation Ruthie had with me many years back about David's taking things from the army.

DEFENSE: Did you have any further conversations with David Greenglass?

JULIUS: He called me up and said "It's very urgent, I have got to see you." . . . A day or two after that . . . I dropped in at his house. Dave was very excited. He was pale and he had a haggard look on his face.

DEFENSE: Did you then go out of the house with Davey?

JULIUS: I did.

DEFENSE: Tell us what happened?

JULIUS: Well, . . . as we were walking up the street toward the East River Drive . . . I said to Dave, "You look very agitated. Calm yourself, take it easy. What's troubling you? And he said, "Julie, I am in a terrible jam." I says . . . "I realize you have been asking me for money, you have been telling me to go to my doctor for a certificate, you have been talking about Mexico, what is the trouble Dave?" He said, "I can't tell you everything about it. All I want you to do for me, Julie, is I must have a couple of thousand dollars in cash." I says, David, I don't have the money on me, I can't raise that kind of money." He says, "Julie, can you borrow it from your relatives?" I says, "No, Dave, I can't do that." "Well, Julie, I just got to have that money and if you don't get me that money you are going to be sorry." I said, "Look here, Dave, what are you trying to do, threaten me or blackmail me? Well, he was very excitable at this time, he was puffing and I saw a wild look in his eyes, and I realize it was time to cut this conversation short. I says; "Look, Dave, you go home, take a cold shower, I have some work to do, I am going to the shop, good bye." And I left him at that time.

DEFENSE: Did you give him any money?

JULIUS: I did not give him any money.

DEFENSE crosses down left of JULIUS.

JUDGE: Madam and gentlemen of the jury: You are the exclusive judges of the relative importance and credibility of the witnesses. The defendants are accused of having conspired to commit espionage. Espionage, reduced to essentials, means spying on the United States to aid a foreign power. Because of the development of highly destructive weapons and their highly guarded possession by nations existing in a state of tension with one another, the enforcement of the espionage laws takes on a new significance. Our national well-being; requires that we guard against spying on the secrets of our defense.

This does not mean that the mere allegation or use of the word "espionage" should justify convicting innocent persons; however, irrational sympathies must not shield proven traitors.

The LIGHTS in the courtroom fade out as the LIGHT comes up on JULIUS' cell. DAVID exits with his chair. PROSECUTOR exits, JULIUS stands and walks into his cell. DEFENSE and ETHEL take the 2 chairs center stage facing front. DEFENSE exits. ETHEL stands in front of her chair.

JULIUS: I believe Greenglass did it to save his own skin. . . . With my background of being fired for alleged communism from the government service, because I was a union organizer, and since he was a relative and knew me intimately, and we had violent quarrels and there existed personal animosity between us, I was falsely involved. . . . Greenglass and Gold were together in the Tombs for nine months discussing the case, studying notes from a big loose leaf book, rehearsing testimony, talking to FBI agents, the prosecution and their attorney. . . . The records of the Tombs will show it, and yet (the government) . . . refused to give us an opportunity to subpoena these records to prove this. . . . Greenglass was coached on the A-bomb sketch testimony, both verbally and from notes.

The prosecution permitted the Greenglasses to perjure themselves. . . . In short we did not get a fair trial and we were framed.

LIGHTS fade out on cell and up on courtroom as JULIUS adjusts his tie and walks to his chair in the courtroom. ETHEL and JULIUS stand in front of their chairs center stage. The JUDGE sits on his bench behind them.

NARRATOR'S VOICE: We the jury, find Julius Rosenberg guilty as charged. We, the jury, find Ethel Rosenberg guilty as charged.

JUDGE: I want to say to you . . . members of the jury, that you have my deepest gratitude for the conscientious and industrious way in which you went about deliberating in this case. This case is important to the government of the United States.

My own opinion is that your verdict is a correct verdict. . . . I must say that as an individual I cannot be happy because it is a sad day for America. The thought that citizens of our country would lend themselves to the destruction of their own country by the most destructive weapon known to man is so shocking that I can't find words to describe this loathsome offense.

And I say a great tribute is due to the FBI and Mr. Hoover for the splendid job that they have done in this case.

It is to America's credit that it took the pains and exerted the effort which it did in the trial of these defendants. Yet, they made a choice of devoting themselves to the Russian ideology of denial of God, denial of the sanctity of the individual and aggression against free men everywhere instead of serving the cause of liberty and freedom.

The defendants are American citizens. They profited from our system of higher education. I also assume that the basic Marxist goal of world revolution and the destruction of capitalism was well known to the defendants, if in fact not subscribed to by them when they passed what they knew was this nation's most deadly, and closely guarded secret weapon to Soviet agents. Indeed the defendants Julius and Ethel Rosenberg placed their devotion to their cause above their own personal safety and were conscious that they were sacrificing their own children, should their misdeeds be detected--all of which did not deter them from pursuing their course. Love for their cause dominated their lives--it was even greater than their love for their children.

LIGHTS fade out on courtroom and up on cells. ETHEL and JULIUS cross to their cell. JULIUS takes off his jacket and loosens his tie. ETHEL puts down her purse and takes off her coat and sits on her cot. Theme music comes up softly.

ETHEL: I awoke at 4:30 AM to hear a mouse squeaking almost in my ear, it was so close . . . I could not get back to sleep. Usually I am able to prevent thoughts of the children and our shattered home from taking full possession of me, but today I fought a losing battle.... For several hours I was on an uncontrollable crying jag, and my head felt as though it might burst. My best friend, for whom I had done the very same this morning, ministered to me with cold compresses and stern admonitions to stop crying -- thus causing it to get worse instead of better. As you can see it was just one of those delightful days in jail.

JULIUS: The pictures of our two sons keep flashing through my mind. Denial of family and freedom is tantamount to a living death. . . . Without a doubt, my sweet, when I go to bed you're in my arms and we lock out the bars and the nightmares. But the morning rays of sunshine rudely awaken me and announce my forced separation from you, the love of my life. (JULIUS puts on his jacket and adjusts his tie as ETHEL puts on her coat, hat and purse) Take heart. The future will be wonderful.

ETHEL and JULIUS exit cells turn and cross up to courtroom as lights fade out on cells and up on courtroom. They sit.

JUDGE: I consider your crime worse than murder. I believe your conduct has already caused, in my opinion the Communist aggression in Korea with the resultant casualties exceeding 50,000 and who knows but that millions more of innocent people may pay the price of your treason. Indeed by your betrayal you undoubtedly have altered the course of history to the disadvantage of our country. The punishment to be meted out in this case must therefore serve the maximum interest for the preservation of our society against these traitors in our midst. It is not in my power, Julius and Ethel Rosenberg, to forgive you. Only the Lord can find mercy for what you have done. (ETHEL and JULIUS stand) The sentence of the Court upon Julius and Ethel Rosenberg is, for the crime for which you have been convicted, you are hereby sentenced to the punishment of death,

41

and it is ordered upon some day within the week beginning with Monday, May 21st, you shall be executed according to law.

The JUDGE steps down from his bench and exits. ETHEL and JULIUS sit. After a pause they stand and walk to pools of light behind each of their cells. Court room lights fade out. LIGHTS fade out on ETHEL and JULIUS as the LIGHT fades up dim on NARRATOR who continues with the slide show.

NARRATOR: After the sentencing, Ethel and Julius are taken to separate holding cells in the basement of the Foley Square Courthouse, where they communicate by singing.

ETHEL: (sings Aria from Madame Butterfly)

SOON WE'LL SEE AT DAYBREAK

A TINY THREAD OF SMOKE RISE

WHERE THE SKY BORDERS ON THE OCEAN

AND THEN A SHIP IN MOTION.

JULIUS: (sings)

MINE EYES HAVE SEEN THE GLORY

OF THE COMING OF THE LORD

HE IS TRAMPLING ON THE VINTAGE

WHERE THE GRAPES OF WRATH ARE STORED

HE HAS LOOSED THE FATEFUL LIGHTENING

OF HIS TERRIBLE SWIFT SWORD

HIS TRUTH IS MARCHING ON.

NARRATOR: The Rosenberg's friend and co-defendant, Morton Sobell, receives a sentence of 30 years. Released 18 years later, he still proclaims his and the Rosenberg's innocence. After cooperating with the government, David Greenglass receives an 18 years sentence and is out in eight. Ruth remains free. Protests spring up all over the world. Demonstrations occur in London, in Paris, in Rome, in New York, in Washington D.C. and elsewhere demanding clemency for the Rosenbergs. Their lawyer, Manny Bloch, continues their appeals. None of the later appeals are ever heard on their merits. New evidence that proves government perjury is never permitted to be tested in a court of law. The Supreme Court refuses twice to even look at the case.

LIGHTS go out on Slides and NARRATOR as they fade up on JULIUS in his cell.

JULIUS: Dearest Ethel, Manny is truly a jewel. All power to him as he is doing a magnificent job. Take heart and know that we are not alone. The monstrous sentence passed on us, which at first stunned the people, will, as time goes on result in an avalanche of protest and this great movement, coupled to our legal fight, will set us free. Certain things I will not put in letters but leave for our attorneys to convey to you by word of mouth. You understand the American Gestapo is all "eyes and ears" in their drive to establish thought control over the people. The "loyalty" oaths, political frame-up trials through which they parade perjured stool pigeons and witch hunt to shackle the minds of the American nation.

NARRATOR: Julius is transferred to Sing Sing Prison. The Rosenbergs spend the remaining two years of their lives in the Death House.

JULIUS: The only documentary evidence produced by the Government to tie us up with this case was a tin collection can. "Save a Spanish Republican Child." This can was supposed to be used to collect funds to aid the innocent victims of the fascist butcher Franco . . . . I remember when the rebellion broke in Spain and my wife and I decided to help them.

LIGHT fades up dimly on ETHEL sitting on the cot in her cell. She hums "No Pasaran."

JULILUS: Ethel sings beautifully. Together with a few of our friends we went to Times Square on Saturday night. Ethel sang two Spanish songs and No Pasaran and the rest of us held the corners of a Spanish Republican flag.

LIGHT fades up full on ETHEL as light dims on JULIUS.

ETHEL: (sings "No Pasaran")

OH THEY GO SINGING

OH THEY GO MARCHING

YES THEY ARE FIGHTING FOR YOU AND ME

YES THEY ARE FIGHTING TO CRUSH ALL TRAITORS

THAT FRANCO'S POWER SHALL NEVER BE

THE FASCIST BOMBERS THE FASCIST BULLETS

THEY LEAVE OUR CITIES A SMOKING MASS

THEY WANT TO PLUNDER AND RULE OUR COUNTRY

BUT AT MADRID - NO PASARAN

(SPOKEN) THEY SHALL NOT PASS.

NARRATOR: Ethel is the only woman in the empty women's section of the Sing Sing Death House.

ETHEL: I am sealed in the gray walls of this prison as if in a tomb. I am alone in an entire building except for the matron who guards me. I see no other human being from morning to night and from night to morning. I have no occupation other than to sit immured in the aching soundlessness of my narrow cell. I have no recreation other than to walk on a bare patch of ground, surrounded by walls so high that my only view is a bare patch of sky. Sometimes I can see an airplane passing by; sometimes, a few birds; sometimes, I hear the noise of a train in the distance. Otherwise, there is always dead silence.

NARRATOR: Tessie Greenglass sends a telegram to her daughter, Ethel. "Dear Ethel, went to see children last Sunday and saw them twice during the week but; they didn't see me. They were crying steadily. Would come to see you but would not be able to take it. All broken up with heartache. Let me hear from you. Love mother.

LIGHT fades out on NARRATOR.

ETHEL: My heart aches for the children. It is for them I am most concerned and it is of their reaction I am anxiously awaiting some word. . . . My emotions are in storm, as your own must be. Courage darling, there's much to be done.

NARRATOR'S VOICE: Ethel and Julius see their children for the first time, one year after their arrest.

LIGHT fades up on JULIUS standing in his cell. LIGHT on ETHEL remains up. She sits on her cot.

JULIUS: After lunch I went into the counsel room and the kids were hiding behind the door. When I hugged them they seemed so small and far away. I was a bit dazed. I choked up and my eyes teared and Michael kept repeating, Daddy, your voice has changed. After a couple of minutes I was back on an even keel. A round of kissing and hugging and then Robby sat on my lap. Thin face, ringed eyes, looked up at me and he said, "Daddy, why you no come home?" I carefully explained. He replied, "Why did you not visit us Sundays at the Shelter" Again I explained. . . . Darling, the children need us and I hope it is not much longer that we will suffer such anguish being separated from them. . . . After I left them, I felt I tore out a piece of my heart.

ETHEL: My dearest love, as I smiled and kissed the children, I was experiencing such a bewildering assortment of emotions that I don't think I was enough in control of myself to have accomplished anything very far reaching. (she stands) Actually, I doubt anyone else could have either; after all, a first visit after a year's separation can hardly be expected to do much more than 'break the ice.'

JULIUS: (walks in his cell) My Dearest Sweetheart, I held Robby close, kissed him and carried him around so I could talk to Michael. Much of the hour was spent in discussion of the death sentence, which he said he read about in the paper. I told him we were not concerned about it, that we were innocent and we had many avenues of appeal and that it was not his job to be concerned about it but to grow up and be well. He asked me how you die and I told him and he asked if there is an electric chair here and I said yes. He kept on asking about the appeals and what if finally we might lose. Then death faced us. I kept on assuring him but I could see he was terribly upset over it. (He turns front)

My Dearest Son Michael, For me your visit was wonderful. It made me happy to hold you in my arms and kiss you. . . . I want to tell you that I am confident in the end we will be set free because Mommy and I are innocent and we will fight in every possible way and through the courts to win our freedom as soon as possible.

ETHEL: Dearest children: The snow is whirling outside my window as I sit at my writing table and wonder what my darlings might be doing at this moment. The other day, when I was outside in the yard, the snow that had fallen the night before looked so much like the icing on a birthday cake that I couldn't resist printing letters in it with my right foot. By the time I was through, all our initials were outlined clear, MR, RR, ER and JR. Do you remember how we used to tease Daddy by calling him JR the wonder dog?

She sits on her cot.

JULIUS: (sits on his cot facing towards ETHEL'S cell) Oh joy of joy I caught a couple of bars of your rendition of "Ave Maria" and the "Alleluia." Imagine if only your door were open, what a lovely concert we would have. I reminisced a bit of the many times you would sing my favorite arias and folk tunes. (ETHEL lies down) Honey, as I thought of it I just adored you. Too bad you weren't closer. I'm sure I would have conveyed my deepest feelings for you in a way that is very: proper indeed for two lovebirds! I send you my tender kisses as messages of my heart.

ETHEL sits up on her cot. JULIUS turns front.

JULIUS: May 31, 1953, Ethel Darling, What does one write to his beloved when faced with the very grim reality that in eighteen days, on their fourteenth wedding anniversary, it is ordered that they be put to death?

ETHEL: (stands and walks forward) Dear Manny: Just as I was sitting down to lunch, Mr. Bennett entered the women's wing of the Death House and announced himself. Contrary to all established practice, he was alone with me. Mr. Bennett came right to the point, he could make available to me any official to whom I might care to divulge espionage information I had hitherto withheld. If I cooperated in this fashion, the Government stood ready to invalidate the death penalty. I made it short and sweet. I was innocent, my husband was innocent and neither of us knew anything about espionage. . . . In order to cooperate as you desire I should have to deliberately concoct a pack of lies and bear false witness against unoffending individuals. Is that what the authorities want me to do '-- to lie? We will not be intimidated by the growing use of undemocratic threat of electrocution . . . , nor will we encourage the undemocratic police state methods by accepting a shabby contemptible little deal in lieu of the justice that is due us as citizens. That is for Hitler Germany, not for the land of liberty. . . . Let me say to you in all sobriety, you will come to me at ten minutes of 11 PM on Thursday, June 18th and the fact of my innocence will not have changed in the slightest.

JULIUS: (stands) Dear Manny, After reading the bald lie of the Justice Department that Mr. Bennett's visit was routine and that they intimated no deal was offered, I feel it my duty to present the facts as they took place last Tuesday Mr. Bennett opened the conversation and said: "Mr. Brownell, the Attorney General, sent me to see you and he wants you to know that if you want to cooperate with the government you can do so through me... If you, Julius, can convince the official that you have fully cooperated with the government, they have a basis to recommend clemency." I said that in the first place, we were innocent, that is the whole truth and therefore we know nothing.... You mean to tell me, Mr. Bennett, I said, that a great government like ours is coming to two insignificant people like us and saying, "cooperate or die"?

ETHEL: Dear Manny, This is to let you know my mother was here on Monday. . . . I pointed out to her that whatever unfortunate fear of reprisal Davy might be harboring, it was my life that was in peril, not him--and further, if I while awaiting electrocution, was not afraid to continue to assert my innocence and give the lie to his story, why couldn't he, in a far more advantageous position, be man enough to own up at long last, to this lie, and help to save my life, instead of letting it be forfeited to save his face! Said she, "So what would have been so terrible if you had backed up his story?" --I guess my mouth kind of fell open. "What," I replied, "and take the blame for a crime I never committed, and allow my name and my husband's and children's to be blackened to protect him? What, and go along with a story that I knew to be untrue, where it involved my husband and me?" . . . Believe it or not she answered , "Yes, you got me straight: I mean even if it was a lie, all right, so it was a lie, you should have said it was true anyway. You think that way you would have been sent here? No, if you had agreed that what Davy said was so, even if it wasn't, you wouldn't have got this!" I protested, shocked as I could be. "But, Ma, would you have had me willingly commit perjury?" She shrugged her shoulders indifferently and maintained doggedly, "You wouldn't be here!"

NARRATOR'S VOICE: They did not cooperate and clemency was denied.

ETHEL and JULIUS walk out of their cells to the space in between. They stand together.

ETHEL: Dear Manny, The following letter is to be delivered to my children.

Dearest Sweethearts, my most precious children, Only this morning it looked like we might be together again after all. Now that this cannot be, I want so much for you to know all that I have come to know. Unfortunately, I may write only a few simple words; the rest your own lives must teach you, even as mine taught me. At first, of course, you will grieve bitterly for us but you will not grieve alone. That is our consolation and it must eventually be yours. Eventually, too, you must come to believe that life is worth living. Be comforted that even now, with the end of ours slowly approaching, that we know this with a conviction that defeats the executioner!

JULIUS: Your lives must teach you, too, that good cannot really flourish in the midst of evil; that freedom and all the things that go to make up a truly satisfying and worthwhile life, must sometimes be purchased very dearly. Be comforted then that we were serene and understood with the deepest kind of understanding, that civilization had not as yet progressed to the point where life did not have to be lost for the sake of life; and that we were comforted in the sure knowledge that others would carry on after us.

ETHEL: We wish we might have had the tremendous joy and gratification of living our lives out with you. . . . Always remember that we were innocent and could not wrong our conscience. We press you close and kiss you with all our strength.

Julius: Daddy and Ethel: Mommy.

LIGHTS dim onstage as ETHEL and JULIUS turn and walk toward the judge's bench, they separate and walk offstage as NARRATOR speaks.

NARRATOR'S VOICE: Two FBI men stood at a telephone line in the prison going to the U.S. Attorney General in Washington, D.C. They were waiting for last minute confessions as the Rosenbergs were taken to the electric chair.

CONSODINE enters walks downstage center between the two cells

BOB CONSODINE: (reporting) They died differently, gave off different sounds, different grotesque manners. Uh -- he died quickly, there didn't seem to be too much life left in him when he entered behind the rabbi. He seemed to be walking in a cadence of steps of just keeping in time with the muttering of the Twenty-third Psalm. Never said a word. Never looked like he wanted to say a word. She died a lot harder. When it appeared that she had received enough electricity to kill an ordinary person and had received the exact amount that had killed her husband, the doctors went over to her and looked at each other rather dumbfounded and seemed surprised that she was not dead. And she was given more electricity which started again the kind of a ghastly plume of smoke that rose from her head. After two more little jolts, Ethel Rosenberg was dead. (He exits left)

LIGHTS fade out.

END

THE STORY OF ETHEL AND JULIUS ROSENBERG

A Courtroom and Prison Drama Set in the 1950's in New York City.

By
Nina Serrano
Paul Richards
Judith Binder

Revised by
Jacob Justice
2016

ISBN 978-0-9972170-3-2 print
ISBN 978-0-9972170-4-9 eBook

Cover art and title page art by Beryl Landau

Cover and book design by Paul Richards

Twenty First Century Revival of *The Story of Ethel and Julius Rosenberg*

Forty years passed after the 1976 closing night performance of *The Story of Ethel and Julius Rosenberg* in San Francisco, California. The script had gone into the file cabinet until 2013, when co-author Paul Richards rediscovered it, digitized it and put it on my website, ninaserrano.com. Three more years went by before we received a surprising email from Jacob Justice of Bryan, Texas seeking authorization for a new 21st century production of T*he Story of Ethel and Julius Rosenberg* at Bryan High School where Jacob is a theater teacher. We were delighted and thrilled to agree.

Jacob did a great job of revising the script by eliminating the narrator to create more action and roles. He added reporters and newsboys shouting out headlines

Jacob Justice and Nina Serrano, Bryan Texas,
2016. Photo by Valerie Landau

and distributed the narrators lines among the cast. Students performed the play November 8, 9, 10 and 11, 2016, including two shows on the final night. My daughter, Valerie Landau, and I were in the audience opening night, November 8, 2016, the night Donald Trump was elected.

I was excited to be there. No matter that the actors were teenagers in a small Texas town, and the Rosenbergs New York City Jews in their late thirties. Right from the airport, I found the people warm and friendly and this high school was no different in spite of my fears about Texas that included horrific tales of the Klu Klux Klan, the Alamo, and lynching.

I met Jacob the day we arrived in Bryan at our motel. He was an intelligent man full of energy and ideas on his lunch break.

"What made you choose this play?" I blurted out, in the motel lobby.

"I like to direct shows about important themes during the school year. In the summer I might consider Disney. But during school I only want plays that matter."

"How did you find our play?" I ventured, delving further into the questions that my co-playwright and husband Paul Richards and I had been asking ourselves for months.

"Last year in the middle school library where I was teaching, I found a book about the Rosenberg case. I picked it up. It fascinated me, reading and re-reading it over the next days. Soon, I knew I wanted to direct a play about this next year at my new job at the high school. I thought it was probably impossible to find a play about the famous spy case of the 50's but I googled it anyway.

'Play about Ethel and Julius Rosenberg.' Up pops your play. It said, 'Estuary Press' which I had never heard of, and 'Contact us.' I wrote off a quick email."

I have recently got a copy of your play of the above name and am enthralled with it. I am a high school theatre teacher in Texas and would love to look into the possibility of performing this show. Each year we have a One Act Play Contest in the State of Texas and I think this story would be a great story to tell.

While I very much enjoyed the play, I was wondering if you would be open to me creating more action in lieu of the narration. There are many parts narrated that I believe could enhance the play if shown to the audience. If this meets with your approval I could begin working on the additions and send them to you for approval.

We agreed instantly to his request to make some revisions. Over the summer he wrote the adaptation.

"Did you like my revisions?" Jacob asked worriedly in the motel lobby.

"We loved it. All that action," I reassured him. "We asked ourselves, Why didn't we think of that?"

Jacob hurried back for his next class, and a pre-opening reception for the cast and crew now getting ready for the premier performance. Valerie and I joined him there where for the first time I met the actors and crew. They had been rehearsing the play and studying the events and characters for the past 5 weeks in their history classes. I pondered on how art crosses generations and geography. Thank goodness for Internet.

As I walked into the school's theatre department, the actors, in make up and costume, tech crew, and some parents, burst into applause. I applauded back. It was a love-fest. The students were so excited to meet the playwright as they were about to perform the play. I was thrilled meeting the young artists who were bringing our play to life again.

Some parents had come to pitch in to help Jacob and support the kids. There was tray of elaborately iced cupcakes. After we exchanged greetings, I was given a lovely gift-- a beautifully decorated Texas boot ornament. I meet each participant, while Valerie snapped photos. The kids dove into the cupcakes.

That night, Valerie and I entered the newly built empty back box theatre with rows of seats on 3 sides. Jacob had mentioned that the theatre for several years had been used as a supply closet. He, the students, and parents had emptied it, painted the floors and walls black, and sewn and hung curtains. The school had bought 100 new chairs. We were the first to sit in them. I explored the court room set, a series of rectangular platforms Jacob and the students had built of wood and covered with newsprint. The theatre felt cold and I waited nervously for other bodies to arrive and warm the place up.

It was election night. I wondered who the audience would be. We had voted by mail earlier in California. Was Texas a red state? Would they boo the play? Run us out of town for corrupting their children with radical ideas? I wasn't concerned with election because it was a sure thing in my mind that Hillary Clinton would win and everything would be the same old, same old. War and more war.

The audience began trickling in--students, staff, parents, young siblings and grandparents. Jacob had said that the community and administration had supported the play. Local businesses contributed money and one thrift store donated the costumes. A student actor who played Ethel's mother Tessie had been the costumer. Since I had played Ethel in the 1976 production, I did take note that the costumes were color coordinated. Ethel and Julius opened in white. David Greenglass, the villainous brother and his wife Ruth and his mother, Tessie, were all in black and white. Once again I wondered why didn't we think of that?

The seats filled. I decided I would attend all five performances and sit in a different area each night, with an entirely different view of the action. Then the house lights came down, stage lights up and music and sound filled the room. I was still moved by the familiar sound of my brother Philip Serrano's Rosenberg theme music. The actors began and from the first moment I could breathe freely. They were so good, so real, and so committed to the truth of their characters.

Jacob had to incorporate more actors into the play because so many students, more girls than boys, had wanted to be in it. Back in 1976, we had tried to keep the cast small and economical.

In Jacob's version, all the actors stepped out of their characters and, except for Ethel and Julius, became the jury sitting on the low benches that defined the courtroom. The jury also served as a Greek chorus. Jacob's addition of the jury encouraged the audience to weigh the facts of the case and intensified the courtroom atmosphere. This device followed Bertold Brecht's technique of distancing the audience from the melodrama.

Jacob added innovative features that enhanced the dramatic action by highlighting the political persecution prevalent during the 1950s. Newspaper sellers ran in shouting out the headlines of the day. Surprisingly, through the use of lighting effects, the back wall of the courtroom suddenly became the judge's bench with the judge appearing above it. Below it we could see and hear a radio announcer's commentary through a scrim that turned translucent when backlit. Sometimes the Ethel and Julius characters would appear and read their heart wrenching letters. Sometimes we would see them respond to their own prerecorded words mixed with music. Other times, after one of Julius or Ethel's readings or David and Ruth Greenglass' scenes, the actors dropped their roles, looked at the audience and filled us in on the historical

Nina Serrano on the set of Bryan High School
Production of The Story Of Ethel and Julius Rosenberg.
Bryan, Texas, 2016.

background with the narrators lines from the original production.

The Rosenberg's letters written from the death house in the anguish of separation from each other and their young children were palpable, especially with the three sided seating bringing the actors and audience into close proximity. So when the actors dropped their roles to speak directly to the audience, it required a shift in the viewer to suspend the vicarious emotional suffering and to engage intellectually with facts.

In our original script, we only used Ethel and Julius's actual letters and words selected from the one thousand page trial transcript and other primary sources. But in Jacob Justice's version, he not only added some new lines of his own, but he also incorporated the new information about the deal David Greenglass had made with FBI to lie about his sister so they could get their conviction. His treachery was publicly revealed years after he got out of prison in 1960, after serving nine and a half years from his original eighteen year sentence. In a 2008 book and interview by NY Times reporter Sam Roberts, Greenglass admitted he had lied about Ethel. The actor portraying him dealt with the man's complexity and had studied him well.

Only a week or two before the 2016 performance of the play, *60 Minutes* had aired a CBS TV program on the Rosenberg case featuring their now grown sons, Robert and Michael Meeropol. The program included footage of the real David Greenglass explaining to the *60 Minutes* reporter how he had no regrets in lying about Ethel because he saved his wife, the mother of his children.

After we left the theatre, our excitement about the play quickly turned into shock as we learned of Trump's election victory. We had been smothered in kindness and appreciation by the cast, crew and their families, and impressed with their deeply felt portrayal of the trial and execution of the Rosenbergs. Now, the election results stood in stark contrast. How could we understand the two events on the same night? We are still pondering that question in 2018.

The new information presented in the play from Sam Roberts book and the CBS interviews with the sons and with FBI informant David Greenglass included allegations linking Julius Rosenberg with Russian spying. But these allegations, made 55 years after the trial, do not change the fact that no evidence was submitted to the court to prove their crime. And nothing changed the fact that there were no atomic bomb secrets in the first place because the science of atom bombs was well known internationally. And certainly the new information that David Greenglass had lied strengthened the case that Ethel was railroaded. We stand behind the play's reliance upon the actual words of the Rosenbergs during that terrible ordeal in which they refused to give false testimony demanded by their inquisitors and went to their deaths proclaiming their innocence.

Why offer *The Story of Ethel and Julius Rosenberg* again after all these years? It has become shockingly clear that their story is more relevant than ever. US government attacks on dissenters and the press, along with the prosecution of wars abroad continue unabated. Chelsea (Bradley) Manning was punished after blowing the whistle on crimes being committed by the US government in Iraq.

Julian Assange of Wikileaks faces the draconian attempt by the US to extradite him to face charges of sedition and treason for exposing crimes hidden by our National Security State. The same lies and techniques used to kill the Rosenbergs are still operating in plain sight. The fight for truth and transparency in government today must not ignore the lessons of the past. The legacy of the Rosenbergs in standing up against government lies based on hidden classified documents, even at the cost of their lives and the orphaning of their children, needs to be heard today if we are ever going to move forward towards a more democratic world.

The Story of Ethel and Julius Rosenberg (2016)

A courtroom and prison drama set in the 1950's in New York City.

Most of the dialogues are direct quotes excerpted from actual transcripts of the Rosenberg's famous trial and their own letters.

Cast of CHARACTERS

Ethel Rosenberg - F

Julius Rosenberg - M

David Greenglass - M

Ruth Greenglass - F

Tessie Greenglass - F

The Defense - M

The Prosecution - M

Sam Roberts -M

Senator Taft -M

Lawyer -M/F

Judge/ President Truman - M

Newsboy 1 -M/F

Newsboy 2 - M/F

Agent 1 - M/F

Agent 2 - M/F

Agent 3 - M

Mr. Bennett - M

Harry - M

Radio Reporter - M/F

Stenographer - F

Note: The character of the DEFENSE is the composite dialogues of Alexander and Emmanuel Bloch. The PROSECUTION is the composite of Roy Cohn and Irving Saypol.

The play is performed without an intermission.

The Set

The room that we are in transforms from a home, to a courtroom, and to a cell. This is best utilized by a unit set. For the audience's clarity, once a location is defined (ex. the judge's bench is upstage center) then continue to use that location for that role where the play allows. The set remains the same throughout the play.

Theme Music

Composed by Philip Serrano. (To hear the music, go to https://www.youtube.com/watch?v=IdKJ8H0FY9c.)

Costumes

All the characters are dressed in clothes of the late 1940's and early 1950's. Costume pieces should be added and taken away if characters change or the passage of time. Keep it simple, especially for quick changes.

Narration

Ethel, Julius, David, and Ruth all act as Narrator's throughout the show, stepping out of the scene to address the audience directly. As Ruth and David's story is used by the prosecution, they take over the narration, as if they are taking over the Rosenberg's story.

Newsboys

The Newsboys can be placed at different locations throughout the theatre. They exist to give the audience a sense of time passing.

Reporter

The Reporter should be used as a broadcast reporter, preferably radio broadcast. This should be a piece of set that doesn't change, preferably above where the action is.

David

David begins and ends the show in his late 70's. The rest of the show he is in his 30's

SLIDE SHOW

In the original production, there were 80 slides. If you wish to utilize these in this show, you may use them during Ethel, Julius, David, or Ruth's Narration throughout the show. The Narrator operated the slide machine to illustrate the narration. Photos were found in newspapers and magazines from the Rosenberg's arrest in June 1950 to their execution in June, 1953. Highly recommended sources of photographs are:

We Are Your Sons by Michael and Robert Meeropol, Houghton-Mifflin, 1975, and University of Illinois Press, Subsequent Edition, 1986.

Invitation to An Inquest by Walter and Miriam Schnier, Pantheon Books, 1983.

The Unquiet Death of Ethel and Julius Rosenberg, by Alvin H. Goldstein, Lawrence Hill Books, 1975.

LIGHTS

The lights indicate the location of the action, e.g. on courtroom, jail cots, etc.

THE PLAY

The stage is set to use unit pieces and movable set pieces to create different places. At the top of the show there is a table and two chairs.

DAVID hears knocking. He is dressed as an older man; in a weak voice.

DAVID: Yes, who is it?

SAM: It's Sam Roberts, the reporter, mind if we finish up today?

DAVID: Yes, come in, come in.

Sam enters

DAVID: I wish you would have never found me. (Freeze)

JULIUS: (Appears DSL, aside) Tonight you are here to hear our story, I am Julius. (move to USL)

SAM: (scene comes to life) Well... I did find you. All we need is some final thoughts and then we can finish the story.

DAVID: (thinking) And I still get paid?

SAM: Yes.

DAVID makes a motion with his hands as if the matters settled.

DAVID: Sit, sit.

SAM begins getting out recorder and paper/pen.

SAM: Can you tell me more about your sister and her husband? (Freeze)

ETHEL: (Appears DSR) I am Ethel, and we are the Rosenberg's. Tonight you will hear our story. (Move to USR)

DAVID unfreezes, looks away, distant. Julius and Ethel, lights up on their silhouettes on opposite sides of the stage US, they begin moving towards each other to dance. She loved him.

SAM: Mr. Greenglass, I know this will be hard, but why did you do what you did?

DAVID: (pause) My wife is more important to me than my sister. Or my mother or my father, OK? And she was the mother of my children.

LIGHTS transition as scene moves away from the room and into the courtroom, JULIUS and ETHEL continue dancing downstage as court scene begins.

DEFENSE: What is your full name?

The couple are interrupted in their dance. They open up with one arm still around the other.

JULIUS responds to the questions. MUSIC cuts off, as music cuts off their smiles to turn firm and stern looks as they slowly move from arms around each other to holding hands.

JULIUS: Julius Rosenberg.

DEFENSE: And how old are you?

JULIUS: 33.

DEFENSE: Where were you born?

JULIUS: I was born in New York City.

NEWSBOY 1: (Appears) August 6, 1945. US drops atomic bombs on Japan! Get 'ya papes today!

DEFENSE: And were you educated here in New York City?

JULIUS: Yes I was. At the same time that I attended Public school I attended Hebrew School. I entered the School of Technology of the College of the City of New York in June 1934 and I attained my degree of a Bachelor of Electrical engineering in February of 1939.

NEWSBOY 2: (Appears) Extra! Extra! World War 2 big 3 alliance between the U. S., Brits and Russia has broken up.

DEFENSE: To whom are you married?

Lights change, Julius moves to "letter" spot.

JULIUS: (Writing) Dearest wife and two boys, I am allowed to send you three letters a week. This afternoon before supper I had a talk with the visiting Rabbi. He's a nice guy and if the front office will permit him, he will call Mom and tell her I'm alright. I hear your brother David was shipped off to the tombs.

Lights change to courtroom.

JULIUS: I am married to Ethel Rosenberg.

DEFENSE: Now, is she the lady who was sitting next to you at the counsel table and is sitting right now here?

JULIUS: Yes, Sir.

He turns to ETHEL, takes her in his arms and they continue to dance. Music fades in. The DEFENSE walks in the darkness, circling around in the darkness upstage behind Ethel.

NEWSBOY 1: Cold war confrontation between countries.

REPORTER: U.S. foreign policy Anti-Communism and nuclear monopoly dominates U.S. foreign policy.

The stage comes to life. The DEFENSE's question again interrupts the dance. Ethel spins to the witness stands while Julius remains standing stage left, watching.

DEFENSE: (to Ethel) Are you married?

ETHEL: Yes

DEFENSE: To whom?

ETHEL: Julius Rosenberg.

Ethel moves to "letter" spot. Lights change.

ETHEL: (Writing) Dearest Julie. This will have to be brief as it is now close to 1:00 AM and my eyes ache for lack of sleep. Just got through hanging the clothes as Mike didn't get off to sleep until 11:30. Have an awful lot scheduled before I see you again. The accountant is coming in Thursday. Received a number of bills, two of which are telephone bills. How long can I wait to pay bills? Love you darling" miss you and can't wait until Sunday, when I'll be able to visit you--in prison. I can't believe it yet.

Ethel moves back to stand, lights change to courtroom.

DEFENSE: The other defendant in this case?

ETHEL: That is right.

DEFENSE: And you are a defendant in this case?

ETHEL: Yes, I am.

NEWSBOY 1: (appears) This just in, Seven Chicago scientists claim the Soviet Union can build the bomb!

NEWSBOY 2: (appears) The Soviets have the technology and the facilities to produce the bomb!

DEFENSE: What was your maiden name?

ETHEL: Ethel Greenglass.

DEFENSE: How many brothers and sisters have you?

ETHEL: I have three brothers... David, Bernard and Sam.

DEFENSE: How many children have you?

ETHEL: I have two children... Michael was eight March tenth and Robert will be four, May eleventh.

ETHEL and JULIUS move to "letter" spot. Lights change.

ETHEL: Dearest Sweethearts, my most precious children...

JULIUS: Your lives must teach you, too, that good cannot really flourish in the midst of evil . . .

ETHEL: I may only write a few simple words . . .

JULIUS: That freedom and all the things you go to make up a truly satisfying and worthwhile life. . .

ETHEL: You must come to believe that life is worth living.

JULIUS: Must sometimes be purchased very dearly.

ETHEL: We press you close and kiss you with all our strength.

ETHEL turns to JULIUS and goes into his arms. They continue dancing to the theme music which has faded up. They dip and turn playfully, enjoying the intimacy as if dancing in their own living room. Dim LIGHT fades, ETHEL AND JULIUS freeze in their dance and ETHEL walks downstage stopping at center to address the audience.

ETHEL: (addressing audience) In 1947, the Taft Hartley act was drafted with the goal of putting legal limitations on the worker's rights to organize and make it illegal for Communists to hold Union office. It passes both the Senate and the House and lands on the President's desk

TRUMAN: To the House of Representatives: I return herewith, without my approval, H.R. 3020...

NEWSBOY 1: June 20, 1947! President Truman Vetoes the Taft-Hartley Act!

TRUMAN: I share with the Congress the conviction that legislation dealing with the relations between management and labor is necessary.

REPORTER: President Truman's administration has been quiet on the Taft- Hartley Act leading up to his veto. But now the President has sent a letter to Congress. TRUMAN: This bill is far from a solution. This is a critical period in our history, and any measure which will adversely affect our national unity will render a distinct disservice not only to this nation but to the world. I am convinced that such would be the result if the veto of this bill should be overridden.

JULIUS: (addressing audience)The Taft- Hartley Act banned closed shops for strikes, permitted the president to order cooling off periods before strikes in certain industries, and reduced the budget of the Department of Labor.

TRUMAN: One of the major lessons of recent world history is that free and vital trade unions are a strong bulwark against the growth of totalitarian movements. We must, therefore, be everlastingly alert that in striking at Union abuses we do not destroy the contribution which unions make to our democratic strength.

REPORTER: Labor leaders are dubbing this the "slave labor" bill. 28 members of Congress have declared in a new guarantee of industrial slavery. The

Senate is reconvening since Truman's veto to decide the fate of the Taft-Hartley Act. In response to President Truman, Senator Taft argued.

SEN TAFT: There is an unquestioned public demand for labor legislation to end abuses which are apparent to the American people.

NEWSBOY 2: June 23, 1947! Senate overrides labor bill veto!

JULIUS: (addressing audience) Communists and suspected Communists are purged.

LIGHTS transition as ETHEL and JULIUS begin dancing. The THEME MUSIC ends and the MUSIC of UNION MAID comes up. They continue dancing to the livelier music and sing along with it. They waltz and sing as if singing along to the music on the radio.

ETHEL AND JULIUS: (sing)

THERE ONCE WAS A UNION MAID

WHO NEVER WAS AFRAID

OF GOONS AND GINKS AND COMPANY FINKS

AND THE DEPUTY SHERIFFS WHO MADE THE RAIDS

SHE WENT TO THE UNION HALL

WHEN A MEETING IT WAS CALLED

AND WHEN THE LEGION BOYS CAME ROUND

SHE ALWAYS STOOD HER GROUND.

OH, YOU CAN'T SCARE ME

I'M STICKING TO THE UNION

I'M STICKING TO THE UNION

I'M STICKING TO THE UNION

OH, YOU CAN'T SCARE ME,

I'M STICKING TO THE UNION

I'M STICKING TO THE UNION TILL THE DAY I DIE.

They twirl around, laughing. Julius spins Ethel out under his arm. He ends up in front of the two chairs stage left of the Judge's bench. She is stage right of the bench. DEFENSE Enters in the darkness behind them.

DEFENSE: What union did you belong to?

The dance is interrupted. Music stops.

JULIUS: The Federation of Architects and Engineers.

DEFENSE: And what did you do during most of the years in that union in terms of activity?

JULIUS: Well, for a period of time I was chairman of the Federal Civil Service committee of that union.

DEFENSE: And in connection with that activity, did you help members of that union with respect to keeping their positions?

JULIUS: That is correct. DEFENSE: And did you handle grievance cases? JULIUS: Yes.

DEFENSE: For that union? JULIUS: Yes.

As ETHEL and JULIUS turn toward each other, the PROSECUTOR and JUDGE enter in the darkness behind them. the JUDGE sits on his bench. The prosecutor stands opposite Bloch outside the pool of light. ETHEL and JULIUS move toward each other to continue their dance. They are interrupted by the PROSECUTOR.

PROSECUTOR: Is it not a fact that you were removed from government service because you were a member of the Communist party? DEFENSE: If the court please... if the prosecutor wants a concession, I will concede right now that this witness was removed from Government service upon charges that he was a member of the Communist Party.

PROSECUTOR: Were you a member of the Communist Party?

JULIUS: I refuse to answer on the ground that it might incriminate me.

PROSECUTOR exits, JULIUS moves to "letter" spot. Lights change.

JULIUS: The pictures of our two sons keep flashing through my mind. Denial of family and freedom is tantamount to a living death.... Without a doubt, my sweet, when I go to bed you're in my arms and we lock out the bars and the nightmares. But the morning rays of sunshine rudely awaken me and announce my forced separation from you, the love of my life. Take heart. The future will be wonderful.

ETHEL moves to witness stand. Lights change back to courtroom.

DEFENSE: (to ETHEL) What union did you belong to?

ETHEL: I was a member of the ladies auxiliary of the Federation of Architects and Engineers which was my husband's union and I did a lot of typing for them, and when worked at National packing I was a member of a shipping clerks union. When I worked at Bell Textile Company, I was' a member of Local 65 of the United Wholesale and Retail.

DEFENSE: Were you active in the union?

ETHEL: Yes, I was.

POOL OF LIGHT on ETHEL and JULIUS fades out as light fades up on Reporter.

REPORTER: (Bomb explosion) President Truman announced that Russia has the atom's secret and state departments across the globe have trembled. The grim vision of an atomic war is now closer than ever. The US military has top secret scientists working to lead our nation to a place of strength and survival by creating a nuclear monopoly. The UN Assembly has felt the trembles left by the the Soviets when they exploded an atomic bomb. The United Nations is striving towards the worldwide peace. (Bomb explosion) Will man find refuge or destroy himself? Is mankind headed towards a new world, or crumbling the one we have? The answer may lie in 1950.

JULIUS: (addresses audience) The political climate changes to widespread secrecy, security clearance and loyalty oaths. Because of Russia's bomb, the cold warriors insist that the Soviets are only able to do it because the United States secrets have been stolen.

NEWSBOY 1: J. Edgar Hoover on the hunt for Soviet spies!

NEWSBOY 2: Americans! Don't patronize the Reds! You can drive them out, report activity to the FBI.

LIGHT down. LIGHT up on JULIUS AND ETHEL. They open their arms to each other and start to come together to continue their dance. They are interrupted before they reach each other.

DEFENSE: Now did there come a time when you went into business?

JULIUS: In the spring of 1946 we entered into a new partnership.

DEFENSE: And who were the members of the firm?

JULIUS: My brothers-in-law, Bernard Greenglass and David Greenglass, a neighbor, Isidore Goldstein ... and myself.

DEFENSE: And what was the business?

JULIUS: It was a machine shop.

DEFENSE: (to ETHEL) Now, your brother, David Greenglass, was the youngest in the family... and you were 6 years older than he was, and what was the relationship between you throughout the period of your living together in the same household, until you married and after you married?

ETHEL: Well, he was my baby brother.

DEFENSE: Did you treat him as such?

ETHEL: Yes, that is exactly how I treated him.

DEFENSE: Did you love him?

ETHEL: Yes, I loved him very much.

LIGHT out on COURTROOM. ETHEL addresses audience as scene changes to the ROSENBERG'S home.

ETHEL: (Addresses audience) In 1950, my Julius and I live with our two sons, Michael and Robbie in lower income housing in New York City.

JULIUS: Ethel, I'm home!

ETHEL: Coming dear. (Talking offstage) Michael, Robbie, time to clean up for dinner. (Comes in to Julius) How are you?

JULIUS: (somewhat deflated) I'm good (pause) another day at the machine shop.

ETHEL: (moving towards him) You work hard for us.

JULIUS: And yet...(motioning to their surrounds)

ETHEL: Julie, you are too hard on yourself. We are raising our sons with more than you or I had. And that's because of the work you do.

JULIUS: I never dreamed that this is where we would be when I was taking classes at City College. Head full of dreams...

ETHEL: But that dreamer is the man I married. I can still see you, (moving towards him) so strong in the midst of the Depression... standing against those in power.... speaking what they needed to hear. (She walks behind him) My strong, strong man. (Boys making playful noises off stage) I told you boys to clean up!

JULIUS: Boys will be boys. Have you heard from your brother?

ETHEL: Was he not at the shop?

JULIUS: No, we should check on him.

ETHEL: Always looking out for others you are.

JULIUS: And yet I only have eyes for you.

He goes to her, they playfully chase, and then begin dancing. Phone rings.

ETHEL: Yes. . . Wait slow down . . . David's been arrested? By the FBI?

Lights down on house scene, Lights up on News Boy 1.

NEWSBOY 1: (appears) Government rounding up Commie spies.

LIGHT out on NEWSBOY 1. LIGHT up on COURTROOM. JULIUS is on the stand.

DEFENSE: (to JULIUS) In June, 1950, were you interrogated by the FBI?

JULIUS: Yes. Once.

DEFENSE: When?

JULIUS: The morning after the FBI took David Greenglass in custody. They came to my house.

Three men enter, LIGHTS transition to home scene as JULIUS moves to door.

JULIUS: There were three men. They said. . . .

AGENT 1: We are from the FBI. We would like to talk to you.

JULIUS: (at door, without opening) Ethel, do you think I ought to talk to these gentlemen?

ETHEL: You know, if Davey is in some sort of trouble, if you can help my brother, talk to them; maybe you can be of some assistance to them.

JULIUS: I will talk to you gentlemen. Please come in. I need to finish up a few things.

AGENT 2: Alright, now we'd like to ask you...

JULIUS: (exiting) Michael, Robert, time to get dressed.

JULIUS exits. The three men stand awkwardly in the the house.

ETHEL: Well, have a seat if you're staying. I'm just finishing up breakfast, can I get you anything?

AGENT 3: No ma'am, that won't be necessary.

ETHEL: Alright, but the coffee pots full, so you just let me know.

AGENT 3: Will do ma'am.

The three men make a huddle while seated, discussing something with each other, JULIUS enters again, they stand together.

JULIUS: I will be ready, right after I've had my breakfast.

AGENTS sit in unison.

ETHEL: Julie, (hands him coffee) please, help David. (Hands him toast)

JULIUS takes a bite, sips coffee and spits it back out.

JULIUS: You gentlemen, didn't want any coffee?

They shake their heads no.

JULIUS: Smart men, okay I am ready to talk.

AGENT 1: We can't talk here. Would you like to come down to our office and, uh, have a cup of coffee?

LIGHTS transition to courtroom, JULIUS takes his seat.

JULIUS: And I went with the gentlemen of the FBI about 9 o'clock I believe.

DEFENSE crosses downstage left, still outside the pool of light.

DEFENSE: Now tell us what was said by the FBI agents to you and what you said to them, and how long you stayed there.

JULIUS: They started asking questions about what I knew about David Greenglass. First they tried to get my background, what relations I had with him. I gave them my school background, work background and I told them whatever I knew about David Greenglass's education and his work background. . . . At one point in the discussion, I would say it was about two hours after I was there, they said to me,

AGENT 2: Do you know that your brother-in-law said you told him to supply information for Russia?

JULIUS: That couldn't be true... where is David Greenglass? Will you bring him here to let him tell me that to my face?

AGENT 1: What if we bring him here, what will you do?

JULIUS: I will call him a liar to his face because that is not so. Look gentlemen, at first you asked me to come down and get some information concerning David Greenglass. Now you are trying to implicate me in something. I would like to see a lawyer.

JUDGE: And you didn't say anything about David's request for money in May or June of 1950, nor did you tell them the story as I understand it, of David's anticipated thefts from the Army which were related to you by Ruth Greenglass in February, 1945?

JULIUS: (crosses to the judge's bench) No, I didn't tell them, your honor. The way I was brought up, I don't inform on my wife's brother, and whatever he did, I didn't know about and that is for him to decide, for him to answer.

DEFENSE: (to ETHEL) Did you talk to your sister-in-law, Ruth, after the arrest of your brother?

ETHEL: At my mother's house. . . . I says,

LIGHTS transition to home with Ruth.

ETHEL: Look Ruth, I would like to know something; Are you and Davey really mixed up in this horrible mess?

RUTH: What are you asking such silly questions for? He is not guilty and of course I am not guilty and we have hired a lawyer and we are going to fight this case because we are not guilty. Did you think we were?

ETHEL: Look, I really don't know what to think any more. There have been reports in the newspapers about confessions and much as I believed, always believed in Davey, I had to hear it from your own lips. RUTH: Well now you have heard it and it is the truth. Neither of us is guilty.

LIGHTS transition to courtroom.

DEFENSE: That is the last talk you had with her?

ETHEL: That is right.

DEFENSE AND JUDGE exit. Lights go out on ETHEL and JULIUS as they "watch" the scene play out in front of them. David and Ruth enter and sit at the table.

LAWYER: David, Ruth, you've been charged with conspiracy to commit espionage.

RUTH: David. . . . (crumbles into him crying)

DAVID: Well, what do we do?

LAWYER: It's tricky, the conspiracy law allows the government to prosecute someone without having to prove anything but intention to act, rather than the act itself.

RUTH: So they don't have to prove anything?

DAVID: Now that doesn't seem right. . . .

LAWYER: Well, they've actually offered to let you make a deal. . .(they lean in) if you will cooperate with the government prosecutors, they'll take it easy on you and possibly let Ruth go free.

DAVID: (Beat. He looks at Ruth, then to Lawyer) We'll do it.

REPORTER: June 25, 1950, War has broken out in Korea. Our troops are being sent in. We are now at war against Communism in Asia.

NEWSBOY 2: RED KOREAN WAR BREAKS OUT IN SOUTH!

NEWSBOY 1&2: IT'S WAR!

NEWSBOY 1: Truman orders U.S. Air and Navy to fight in aid of Korea!

RUTH: (addresses audience) Patriotism and anti-Communism reach fever pitch. David names Ethel's husband, as a conspirator. Julius is arrested on July 17, 1950.

BANGING on DOOR.

AGENT 1: Open up! We need Mr. Rosenberg.

ETHEL: (opens door slightly) I need to see a warrant!

JULIUS: (entering) What is going...

AGENT 2: (pushing on the door) Open the door ma'am!

JULIUS: You have no right to bang down our door!

ETHEL: Please stop, we have children! I am calling our lawyer!

AGENT 3: (Door is pushed open) Quiet down and get in the other room with the children.

Ethel hesitates.

JULIUS: (quietly) Please, go.

Ethel exits.

AGENT 2: Mr. Rosenberg, you're under arrest!

JULIUS: For what crime have I committed to be treated as .
. .

AGENT 3: QUIET! You commie spy!

JULIUS: Where are you taking me? Please let me see my children.

AGENT 1: You won't be seeing your children ever again! Your heading to New York City Federal Prison. Get him out of here!

They take him out the door, gets out pad of paper,

AGENT 1: (speaks as he writes) Arrest report: Julius arrested. Ethel, his wife, made a typical communist remonstrance demanding a warrant and the right to call an attorney. She was told to keep quiet and get in the other room with the children which she did.

LIGHTS out on Scene. JULIUS move to "letter spot".)

JULIUS: Dearest Ethel, Manny is truly a jewel. All power to him as he is doing a magnificent job. Take heart and know that we are not alone. The monstrous sentence passed on us, which at first stunned the people, will, as time goes on result in an avalanche of protest and this great movement, coupled to our legal fight, will set us free. Certain things I will not put in letters but leave for our attorneys to convey to you by word of mouth. You understand the American Gestapo is all "eyes and ears" in their drive to establish thought control over the people. The "loyalty" oaths, political frame-up trials through which they parade perjured stool pigeons and witch hunt to shackle the minds of the American nation.

LIGHTS down on "letter" spot. go up on RUTH.

RUTH: (addresses audience) David was still in prison. He had spent 9 months in Tombs prison with Harry Gold, another alleged spy who claimed to be the American courier for Klaus Fuchs. Fuchs had been passing information to the Soviets and he never cooperated the stories that Harry Gold had told.

HARRY: David.

DAVID: What is it Gold?

HARRY: They are coming back!

DAVID: Who?

AGENT 1: Why hello boys! Greenglass, are you ready?

DAVID: You must understand, this is a hard decision for me and for my family.

AGENT 1: Oh, I do understand, but this is what's best for you and your family. Just let us know what your brother-in-law is up to.

DAVID: If I do this, will my wife and children be taken care of?

AGENT 1: Of course, I will make sure of it.

DAVID: Okay, yes I am ready to tell the story.

AGENT 1: Come with me.

LIGHT out on cell. LIGHT up on chair stage right of judge's bench. DAVID enters and sits in the chair, the PROSECUTOR enters and stands above DAVID.

AGENT 1: (in the darkness) Do you swear to tell the truth,and nothing but the truth, so help you God?

DAVID: (in the darkness) I do.

LIGHTS up.

PROSECUTOR: Was Ethel present in any of these occasions in 1945?

DAVID: Never.

PROSECUTOR: Did Ethel ever talk to you about it?

DAVID: Never spoke about it to me, and that's a fact. Aside from trying to protect my sister, believe me, that's a fact.

PROSECUTOR exits as LIGHTS go out on stage and up on DAVID.

DAVID: (addressing audience) These are times of hysteria in the United States. Suspicion becomes the mark of the times. The word of brother used against sister is sufficient to convict and execute. The Cold War makes its deepest penetration of American society, inside an American family.

RUTH: (addressing audience) David's changes his story to implicate his sister, and save me. Ethel is arrested one month after her husband.

LIGHT out on DAVID and RUTH. LIGHT up on ETHEL in her jail cell, She is in a prison dress, pacing and singing to give herself courage.

ETHEL: (sings)

> DIE GEDUNKEN SIND FREI
>
> MY THOUGHTS ALWAYS FREE
>
> MY THOUGHTS GIVE ME PLEASURE

MY THOUGHTS WILL NOT CATER TO DUKE OR DICTATOR

AND FREE MEN WILL SING

MY THOUGHTS ALWAYS FREE

SO THROW ME IN JAIL AND CLOSE THE DOOR ON ME

MY THOUGHTS THEY WILL BLOSSOM

LIKE FLOWERS IN SPRINGTIME

AND FREE MEN WILL SING

DIE GEDUNKEN SIND FREI

ETHEL: (speaks while writing) August 12, 1950. My dearest Darling Julie. By now you must know what has happened to me. . . . My heart cries aloud for you and the children and I must confess that my mind does leap ahead to the frightening possibilities for them. . . . Sweetheart, I talk with you every night before I fall asleep and cry because you can't hear me. And then I tell myself that you too must be choking with the same frustration and wondering if I can hear you. Darling, we mustn't lose each other or the children, mustn't lose our identities. I try to think of the good, fine life we have led all these years and I am agonized with my longing to go on leading it. . . . I love you, Ethel.

ETHEL freezes as RUTH appears.

RUTH: (aside) After Ethel's arrest, the children go to the home of Ethel and David's mother, TESSIE Greenglass.

RUTH watches scene with TESSIE.

TESSIE: I can't believe that Julius would bring this trouble on our family. This whole situation could be solved if they would just do what the government wants! Julie brought this on us. . . . (Looking off stage, yelling) ROBBIE, stop that! (To Ruth) These children, there just like their father, don't know how to behave. Why can't they just do what Ruthie did?

Lights change back to Ruthie

RUTH: What Ruthie did. . . . (fighting back tears) I did what I had to for my family!

TESSIE exits. DEFENSE enters in darkness, LIGHT out on RUTH and up on ETHEL in her cell.

DEFENSE: Where are your children now?

ETHEL: They are at a temporary shelter in the Bronx.

DEFENSE: Have you seen them since you were arrested?

ETHEL: No, I have not.

DEFENSE exits. ETHEL moves to "letter" spot. Lights change

ETHEL: Dearest children: The snow is whirling outside my window as I sit at my writing table and wonder what my darlings might be doing at this moment. The other day, when I was outside in the yard, the snow that had fallen the night before looked so much like the icing on a birthday cake that I couldn't resist printing letters in it with my right foot. By the time I was through, all our initials were outlined clear, M.R., R.R., E.R. and J.R. Do you remember how we used to tease Daddy by calling him JR the wonder dog'?

LIGHT out on ETHEL. LIGHT up on REPORTER.

REPORTER: Fight Communism with "Truth Dollars!" Donate today to the anti-communist inquisition! Richard H. Nixon, a young Congressman from California, has joined the prosecution of suspected communists in the State Department. Joseph McCarthy, Senator from Wisconsin, has provided his list of names of reds in the government. Presidents Harry S. Truman and Dwight D. Eisenhower, are swept along by the tide. Patriotism becomes the order of the day.

ACTORS: Stand up and be an American.

ETHEL: (addresses audience) It is implied that the model for Americanism is a the white Anglo-Saxon Protestant who supports business over labor, spending for guns over spending for people and, above all, someone who doesn't question our government's policies at home or abroad. People are convicted, condemned and jailed for their beliefs. The Fifth Amendment echoes in the courtrooms.

JULIUS, ETHEL, DAVID, RUTH: I have a right to remain silent against self-incrimination.

JULIUS: (addresses audience) People are afraid, knowing that if they are suspect, admitting merely to knowing someone makes the other person suspect, too. Many people take the Fifth Amendment so they won't be forced to harm others..

REPORTER: In Asia, China has a successful communist revolution. Civil War breaks out in Korea. Vietnamese, led by Ho Chi Minh fight against French Colonialism. American intervention in Korea is a first step into a costlier even bloodier war in Indo-China. Latin America and Puerto Rican Nationalists demand independence from the U. S.

NEWSBOY 1: 2 die, 3 shot in attempted assassination of President Truman.

REPORTER: A Puerto Rican nationalists attempts to assassinate President Harry S. Truman, in Washington, D.C. In Africa, the black world protests. Independence struggles deepen and bring new independent African nations into being. Black Americans find crosses burning in their yards and are lynched by racist mobs.

NEWSBOY 2: Americans are frightened into building bomb shelters.

REPORTER: Children, rehearse your air raid drills and wear your identification tags in case of war with the Communist Russians!

LIGHT out on REPORTER and NEWSBOYS. LIGHTS fade up dim on the courtroom. PROSECUTOR enters with flag and puts the pole in a stand. DAVID enters and stands in front of his chair. DEFENSE enters and stands next to 2 empty chairs JUDGE enters, steps up on the bench and stands.

DAVID: In this environment, in March, 1951, eight months after their arrest, Ethel and Julius go on trial accused of conspiracy to commit espionage, for stealing the secrets of the atom bomb.

ETHEL and JULIUS rise from their jail cots. They take their coats from under the cots and put them on. ETHEL puts on her hat and picks up her purse as JULIUS puts on his tie and buttons his jacket. They step out into the space between their two cells and face each other. Their wrists are crossed together as if by handcuffs; ETHEL lifts her hands with wrists crossed, to JULIUS' face. He lifts his arms with wrists crossed, over her head and shoulders. They kiss. They come out of their embrace, turn to face the courtroom. Their wrists release as they walk side by side to their chairs. ETHEL is at the chair right. JULIUS is to her left. They turn to face front and stand.

VOICE: (offstage) Judge Irving Kaufman presides.

JUDGE, the ROSENBERGS and DAVID sit.

PROSECUTOR; Ladies and Gentlemen of the jury... the evidence will show that the loyalty of the Rosenbergs was not to this country, but that it was to Communism -- Communism in this country and Communism throughout the world.

DEFENSE: (crosses to the JUDGE) If the court pleases. I object to these remarks. . . because Communism is not on trial here.

JUDGE: The charge here is espionage. It is not that the defendants are members of the Communist Party or that they had any interest in Communism.

However, if the Government intends to establish that they did have an interest in Communism, for the purpose of establishing a motive for what they were doing I will, in due course, when that question arises, rule on that point. . . .

DEFENSE crosses and stands left of JULIUS)

JUDGE: Excuse me, I think I said to the jury that the charge was espionage. I want to correct that. The charge is conspiracy to commit espionage.

PROSECUTOR: (Stands behind DAVID) David Greenglass, have you entered a plea to that indictment. . . . charging conspiracy to commit espionage?

DAVID: I have.

PROSECUTOR: What is that plea?

DAVID: Guilty.

PROSECUTOR: (Crosses to the left of DAVID) Your sister is the defendant, Mrs. Ethel Greenglass Rosenberg, is that correct?

DAVID: That is true.

PROSECUTOR: And another defendant, Julius Rosenberg, is your brother-in-law?

DAVID: That is true.

PROSECUTOR: Now did you have any discussion with Ethel and Julius concerning the relative merits of our form of government and that of the Soviet Union?

DAVID opens his mouth to speak. He is interrupted by DEFENSE.

DEFENSE. (crosses to JUDGE) Objected to as incompetent, irrelevant and immaterial, not pertinent to the issues raised in the indictment and the plea. This will obviously lead to matters which will make it difficult or almost impossible for the jury to confine themselves to the real issues in the case.

PROSECUTOR: (Crosses to JUDGE) Your Honor. Of course the views of the defendants on the relative merits of this country and the Soviet Union are extremely relevant when the charge is conspiracy to commit espionage, in that material would be transferred to the Soviet Union to be used to the advantage of the Soviet Union.

JUDGE: What you are trying to bring out from the witness is the fact that the defendants expressed some form of favoritism to Russia in their discussions?

PROSECUTOR: Exactly, Your honor.

JUDGE: I believe it is relevant . . . Objection overruled.

DEFENSE crosses down left. PROSECUTOR turns to DAVID.

PROSECUTOR: You may now answer.

DAVID: I did have such discussions.

PROSECUTOR: Over what period of time, roughly?

JUDGE: Please speak up Mr. Greenglass.

DAVID: From about 1935 to about 1946.

PROSECUTOR: Talking about Socialism over Capitalism, did they specifically talk about Socialism as it existed in the Soviet Union and Capitalism as it existed here?

DAVID: They did.

PROSECUTOR crosses to the right of DAVID.

PROSECUTOR: Which did they like better? Did they tell you? DAVID: They preferred Socialism to Capitalism,

JUDGE: Which type of Socialism?

DAVID: Russian Socialism?

PROSECUTOR: (Crosses to Julius) Did you do anything else besides talk in respect to your feeling... about the Russian position in the war?

JULIUS: I don't understand what you mean.

PROSECUTOR: Did you ever go out and collect any money for the joint Anti-Fascist Refugee Committee?

JULIUS: I don't recall collecting any money, but I recall contributing money.

PROSECUTOR: (holds up can) Do you remember when the agents arrested you and they took that can out of your house?

JULIUS: That is correct.

PROSECUTOR: And the can reads on the label, "Save a Spanish Republican Child, Volveremos, We will return, joint Anti-Fascist Refugee Committee." and there is a notice on the back that the City of New York permits these cans to be used for solicitation. So that perhaps you did a little more them just contribute.

He turns, puts the can on the JUDGES bench and walks to DAVID.

PROSECUTOR: Did you give to Rosenberg a description of the atom bomb itself?

DAVID: I did.

PROSECUTOR: When did you give the first sketch? The first lens mold sketch?

DAVID: That was in January, 1945.

PROSECUTION: To whom did you give it? DAVID: I gave that to Julius Rosenberg.

PROSECUTOR crosses behind DAVID.

DEFENSE: Mr. Rosenberg, did you ever receive a sketch of a cross section of the atom bomb from David Greenglass or Ruth Greenglass at anytime?

JULIUS: No I did not.

DEFENSE: You received a telephone call from Ruth in February, 1945.

JULIUS: That's right.

DEFENSE: And what did she say to you?

JULIUS: She would like to see me.

DEFENSE: Tell us what happened when you went over to see her.

LIGHTS change to house.

RUTH: Julius, I am terribly worried. David has an idea to make some money and take some things from the Army.

JULIUS: Warn David not to do anything foolish. He will only get himself into trouble.

LIGHTS change to courtroom.

DEFENSE: (crosses to ETHEL) Now, will you give us, as far as you can recollect the substance of what your husband told you and what you told him at the time?

LIGHTS change to house.

JULIUS: (enters home) Ruth is worried about David.

ETHEL: What about?

JULIUS: She said Dave has some crazy notions about making some money, about taking some things.

ETHEL: Well what did you tell her? Did you make sure to tell her to warn him about it, not to do it?

JULIUS: Yes.

ETHEL: Well, all right, then I guess there's nothing to worry about.

LIGHTS change to courtroom. PROSECUTOR crosses to the left of DAVID.

PROSECUTOR: Now will you tell us just what happened, Mr. Greenglass, after you handed the sketch and the descriptive material concerning the atomic bomb to Rosenberg? What did he do, and what did the others there do? (Lights change to house)

DAVID: Well, he stepped into another room and he read it and he came out and he said...

JULIUS enters and moves his mouth but David says the lines.

DAVID: This is very good. We ought to have this typed immediately.

RUTH: We will probably have to correct the grammar involved.

Julius moving his mouth, but David saying the lines.

DAVID: Well I was more interested in writing down the technical phrases of it than in correcting the grammar. Get the bridge table and move it here. (Ethel now moves her mouth, but it is David saying the lines) I will get the typewriter.

LIGHTS change to courtroom.

PROSECUTOR: (crosses up center and turns to ETHEL) Who did the typing, Mr. Greenglass?

JUDGE: Now, Mr. Greenglass, would you please remember to speak up.

DAVID: (beat) Ethel did the typing and Ruth and Julius and Ethel did the correction of the grammar.

DEFENSE: (to JULIUS) Did you ever receive such a report or description in writing?

JULIUS: I did not receive any such description or report.

DEFENSE: (to ETHEL) Did you ever type any such information?

ETHEL: No, I never did.

DEFENSE: Or copy any writing that had been made by your brother in which information concerning the atomic bomb was alluded to?

ETHEL: I never did.

DEFENSE: (crosses to left of JULIUS) Now did you see Dave that month, May, 1950?

JULIUS: Yes, I did. . . . About the middle of May . . . David came to my shop one morning and he said,

LIGHTS change to house.

DAVID: Come on outside, I want to talk to you.

DEFENSE: (crosses behind JULIUS and ETHEL) Tell us about the conversation you had.

DAVID: Julie, you got to get me $2000. I need it at once.

JULIUS: Look, Dave, I just don't have the money. What do you need it for?

DAVID: I need the money. Don't ask me questions.

LIGHTS change to courtroom, back on witness stand.

JULIUS: I recall at the time in my mind the incident--I thought maybe it had something to do with a conversation Ruthie had with me many years back about David's taking things from the army.

DEFENSE: Did you have any further conversations with David Greenglass?

JULIUS: He called me up. . .

DAVID: (DSL on phone) It's very urgent, I have got to see you.

JULIUS: A day or two after that . . . I dropped in at his house. Dave was very excited. He was pale and he had a haggard look on his face.

DEFENSE: Did you then go out of the house with Davey?

JULIUS: I did.

DEFENSE: Tell us what happened?

JULIUS: Well . . . as we were walking up the street toward the East River Drive.

LIGHTS change to outside scene.

JULIUS: You look very agitated. (David paces.) Calm yourself, take it easy. What's troubling you?

DAVID: Julie, I am in a terrible jam.

JULIUS: I realize you have been asking me for money, you have been telling me to go to my doctor for a certificate, you have been talking about Mexico, what is the trouble Dave?

DAVID: I can't tell you everything about it. All I want you to do for me, Julie, is I must have a couple of thousand dollars in cash.

JULIUS: David, I don't have the money on me, I can't raise that kind of money.

DAVID: Julie, can you borrow it from your relatives?

JULIUS: No, Dave, I can't do that.

DAVID: Well, Julie, I just got to have that money and if you don't get me that money you are going to be sorry.

JULIUS: Look here, Dave, what are you trying to do, threaten me or blackmail me?

DAVID begins to grow angrier.

DAVID: Well I should...

JULIUS: Look, Dave, you go home, take a cold shower, I have some work to do, I am going to the shop, good bye.

LIGHTS change to courtroom.

DEFENSE: Did you give him any money?

JULIUS: I did not give him any money.

DEFENSE crosses down left of JULIUS, Light Change as JULIUS addresses audience.

JULIUS: (Addressing audience) I believe Greenglass did it to save his own skin. . . . With my background of being fired for alleged communism from the government service, because I was a union organizer, and since he was a relative and knew me intimately, and we had violent quarrels and there existed personal animosity between us, I was falsely involved. . . . Greenglass and Gold were together in the Tombs for nine months discussing the case, studying notes from a big loose leaf book, rehearsing testimony, talking to FBI agents, the prosecution and their attorney. . . . The records of the Tombs will show it, and yet (the government) . . . refused to give us an opportunity to subpoena these records to prove this. . . . Greenglass was coached on the A-bomb sketch testimony, both verbally and from notes. The prosecution permitted the Greenglasses to perjure themselves. . . . In short we did not get a fair trial and we were framed.

Light Change to courtroom. JULIUS and ETHEL are seated together.

JUDGE: Madam and gentlemen of the jury: You are the exclusive judges of the relative importance and credibility of the witnesses. The defendants are accused of having conspired to commit espionage. Espionage, reduced to essentials, means spying on the United States to aid a foreign power. Because of the development of highly destructive weapons and their highly guarded possession by nations existing in a state of tension with one another, the enforcement of the espionage laws takes on a new significance. Our national well-being; requires that we guard against spying on the secrets of our defense. This does not mean that the mere allegation or use of the word "espionage" should justify convicting innocent persons; however, irrational sympathies must not shield proven traitors .

VOICE: We the jury, find Julius Rosenberg guilty as charged. We, the jury, find Ethel Rosenberg guilty as charged.

JULIUS moves to "letter" spot, ETHEL moves to her cell. Lights Change.

ETHEL: sings "Ave Maria" while Julius reads letter.

AVE MARIA

GRATIA PLENA MARIA

GRATIA PLENA MARIA

GRATIA PLENA AVE,

AVE DOMINUS

DOMINUS TECUM

BENEDICTA TU IMULIERIBUS ET BENEDICTUS

BENEDICTUS FRUCTUS VENTRISTUI,

JESUS AVE MARIA

JULIUS: (listens a few bars, then begins) Oh joy of joy I caught a couple of bars of your rendition of "Ave Maria" and the "Alleluia." Imagine if only your door were open, what a lovely concert we would have. I reminisced a bit of the many times you would sing my favorite arias and folk tunes.

ETHEL lies down.

JULIUS: Honey, as I thought of it I just adored you. Too bad you weren't closer. I'm sure I would have conveyed my deepest feelings for you in a way that is very proper indeed for two lovebirds! I send you my tender kisses as messages of my heart.

ETHEL sits up on her cot. JULIUS turns front.

JUDGE: I want to say to you . . . members of the jury, that you have my deepest gratitude for the conscientious and industrious way in which you went about deliberating in this case. This case is important to the government of the United States. My own opinion is that your verdict is a correct verdict. . . .I must say that as an individual I cannot be happy because it is a sad day for America. The thought that citizens of our country would lend themselves to the destruction of their own country by the most destructive weapon known to man is so shocking that I can't find words to describe this loathsome offense. And I say a great tribute is due to the FBI and Mr. Hoover for the splendid job that they have done in this case. It is to America's credit that it took the pains and exerted the effort which it did in the trial of these defendants. Yet, they made a choice of devoting themselves to the

Russian ideology of denial of God, denial of the sanctity of the individual and aggression against free men everywhere instead of serving the cause of liberty and freedom.

The defendants are American citizens. They profited from our system of higher education. I also assume that the basic Marxist goal of world revolution and the destruction of capitalism was well known to the defendants, if in fact not subscribed to by them when they passed what they knew was this nation's most deadly, and closely guarded secret weapon to Soviet agents. Indeed the defendants Julius and Ethel Rosenberg placed their devotion to their cause above their own personal safety and were conscious that they were sacrificing their own children, should their misdeeds be detected--all of which did not deter them from pursuing their course. Love for their cause dominated their lives--it was even greater than their love for their children.

LIGHTS fade out on courtroom and up on cells. ETHEL and JULIUS are in their cells. JULIUS takes off his jacket and loosens his tie. ETHEL puts down her purse and takes off her coat and sits on her cot. Theme music comes up softly. Lights fade on JUDGE.

ETHEL: I awoke at 4:30 AM to hear a mouse squeaking almost in my ear, it was so close ... I could not get back to sleep. Usually I am able to prevent thoughts of the children and our shattered home from taking full possession of me, but today I fought a losing battle. . . . For several hours I was on an uncontrollable crying jag, and my head felt as though it might burst. My best friend, for whom I had done the very same this morning, ministered to me with cold compresses and stern admonitions to stop crying -- thus causing it to get worse instead of better. As you can see it was just one of those delightful days in jail.

Lights fade up to JUDGE. JULIUS and ETHEL's light grows dim while the Judge is speaking.

JUDGE: I consider your crime worse than murder. I believe your conduct has already caused, in my opinion the Communist aggression in Korea with the resultant casualties exceeding 50,000 and who knows but that millions more of innocent people may pay the price of your treason. Indeed by your betrayal you undoubtedly have altered the course of history to the disadvantage of our country. The punishment to be meted out in this case must therefore serve the maximum interest for the preservation of our society against these traitors in our midst. It is not in my power, Julius and Ethel Rosenberg, to forgive you. Only the Lord can find mercy for what you have done.

ETHEL and JULIUS stand.

JUDGE: The sentence of the Court upon Julius and Ethel Rosenberg is, for the crime for which you have been convicted, you are hereby sentenced to the punishment of death, and it is ordered upon some day within the week beginning with Monday, May 21st, you shall be executed according to law.

The JUDGE steps down from his bench and exits. ETHEL and JULIUS sit. After a pause their lights fade out. LIGHT fades up dim on RUTH.

RUTH: (addressing audience) After the sentencing, Ethel and Julius are taken to separate holding cells in the basement of the Foley Square Courthouse, where they communicate by singing.

Lights up on cells.

ETHEL: (sings Aria from Madame.Butterfly)

SOON WE'LL SEE AT DAYBREAK

A TINY THREAD OF SMOKE RISE

WHERE THE SKY BORDERS ON THE OCEAN

AND THEN A SHIP IN MOTION.

JULIUS: (sings)

MINE EYES HAVE SEEN THE GLORY

OF THE COMING OF THE LORD

HE IS TRAMPLING ON THE VINTAGE

WHERE THE GRAPES OF WRATH ARE STORED

HE HAS LOOSED THE FATEFUL LIGHTENING

OF HIS TERRIBLE SWIFT SWORD

HIS TRUTH IS MARCHING ON.

RUTH: (addressing audience) Co-defendant Morton Sobell receives a sentence of 30 years. Released 18 years later, he still proclaims his and the Rosenberg's innocence. After cooperating with the government,

David receives an 18 years sentence and is out in eight. I remain free.

DAVID: (addressing audience) Protests spring up all over the world. Demonstrations occur in London, in Paris, in Rome, in New York, in Washington D.C. and elsewhere demanding clemency for the Rosenbergs. Their lawyer, Manny Bloch, continues their appeals. None of the later appeals are ever heard on their merits. New evidence that proves government perjury is never permitted to be tested in a court of law. The Supreme Court refuses twice to even look at the case.

LIGHTS go out, then fade up on JULIUS in his cell.

DAVID: (addressing audience) Julie is transferred to Sing Sing Prison. The Rosenbergs husband and wife, spend the remaining two years of their lives in the Death House.

JULIUS: (addressing audience from cell) The only documentary evidence produced by the Government to tie us up with this case was a tin collection called "Save a Spanish Republican Child." This can was supposed to be used to collect funds to aid the innocent victims of the fascist butcher Franco. I remember when the rebellion broke in Spain and my wife and I decided to help them.

LIGHT fades up dimly on ETHEL sitting on the cot in her cell. She hums "No Pasaran".

JULIUS: Ethel sings beautifully. Together with a few of our friends we went to Times Square on Saturday night. Ethel sang two Spanish songs and No

Pasaran and the rest of us held the corners of a Spanish Republican flag.

LIGHT fades up full on ETHEL as light dims on JULIUS.

ETHEL: sings "No Pasaran"

> OH THEY GO SINGING
>
> OH THEY GO MARCHING
>
> YES THEY ARE FIGHTING FOR YOU AND ME
>
> YES THEY ARE FIGHTING TO CRUSH ALL TRAITORS THAT FRANCO'S POWER SHALL NEVER BE
>
> THE FASCIST BOMBERS THE FASCIST BULLETS THEY LEAVE OUR CITIES A SMOKING MASS
>
> THEY WANT TO PLUNDER AND RULE OUR COUNTRY
>
> BUT AT MADRID - NO PASARAN
>
> (SPOKEN) THEY SHALL NOT PASS.

RUTH: (addresses audience) Ethel is the only woman in the empty women's section of the Sing Sing Death House.

ETHEL: (addresses audience) I am sealed in the gray walls of this prison as if in a tomb. I am alone in an entire building except for the matron who guards me. I see no other human being from morning to night and from night to morning. I have no occupation other than to sit immured in the aching soundlessness of my narrow cell. I have no recreation other than to walk on a bare patch of ground, surrounded by walls so high that my only view is a bare patch of sky. Sometimes I can see an airplane passing by; sometimes, a few birds;

sometimes, I hear the noise of a train in the distance. Otherwise, there is always dead silence.

RUTH: (addresses audience) TESSIE sent a telegram to her daughter, Ethel while in prison.

TESSIE: (reads) Dear Ethel, went to see children last Sunday and saw them twice during the week but they didn't see me. They were crying steadily. Would come to see you but would not be able to take it. All broken up with heartache. Let me hear from you. Love mother.

ETHEL: My heart aches for the children. It is for them I am most concerned and it is of their reaction I am anxiously awaiting some word. . . . My emotions are in storm, as your own must be. Courage darling, there's much to be done.

RUTH: (addresses audience) Ethel and Julius see their children for the first time, one year after their arrest.

LIGHT fades up on JULIUS standing in his cell. LIGHT on ETHEL remains up. She sits on her cot.

JULIUS: After lunch I went into the counsel room and the kids were hiding behind the door. When I hugged them they seemed so small and far away. I was a bit dazed. I choked up and my eyes teared and Michael kept repeating, Daddy, your voice has changed. After a couple of minutes I was back on an even keel. A round of kissing and hugging and then Robby sat on my lap. Thin face, ringed eyes, looked up at me and he said, "Daddy, why you no come home?" I carefully explained. He replied,

"Why did you not visit us Sundays at the Shelter" Again I explained... Darling, the children need us and I hope it is not much longer that we will suffer such anguish being separated from them. . . . After I left them, I felt I tore out a piece of my heart.

ETHEL: My dearest love, as I smiled and kissed the children, I was experiencing such a bewildering assortment of emotions that I don't think I was enough in control of myself to have accomplished anything very far reaching. (she stands) Actually, I doubt anyone else could have either; after all, a first visit after a year's separation can hardly be expected to do much more than 'break the ice.'

JULIUS: (walks in his cell) My Dearest Sweetheart, I held Robby close, kissed him and carried him around so I could talk to Michael Much of the hour was spent in discussion of the death sentence, which he said he read about in the paper. I told him we were not concerned about it, that we were innocent and we had many avenues of appeal and that it was not his job to be concerned about it but to grow up and be well. He asked me how you die and I told him and he asked if there is an electric chair here and I said yes. He kept on asking about the appeals and what if finally we might lose. Then death faced us. I kept on assuring him but I could see he was terribly upset over it.

(He turns front) My Dearest Son Michael, For me your visit was wonderful. It made me happy to hold you in my arms and kiss you . . . I want to tell you that I am confident in the end we will be set free because Mommy and I are innocent and we will fight in every possible way and through the courts to win our freedom as soon as possible.

Lights fade to dim then up on ETHEL.

ETHEL: (stands and walks forward) Dear Manny: ...Just as I was sitting down to lunch, Mr. Bennett entered the women's wing of the Death House and announced himself.

MR. BENNETT: Mrs. Rosenberg, I'm here to speak with you for a moment, if that's okay.

ETHEL: That's fine, but shouldn't my lawyer be here?

MR. BENNETT: Mrs. Rosenberg, allow me to get straight to the point. I came here to allow you the chance of telling us any espionage information that you had hither to withheld. If you cooperate in this fashion, the Government stands ready to invalidate the death penalty.

ETHEL: Let me make this short and sweet. I am innocent, my husband is innocent and neither of us knows anything about espionage. . . . In order to cooperate as you desire I should have to deliberately concoct a pack of lies and bear false witness against unoffending individuals. Is that what the authorities want me to do '-- to lie? We will not be intimidated by the growing use of undemocratic threat of electrocution . . . , nor will we encourage the undemocratic police state methods by accepting a shabby contemptible little deal in lieu of the justice that is due us as citizens. That is for Hitler Germany, not for the land of liberty. . . . Let me say to you in all sobriety, you will come to me at ten minutes of 11 PM on Thursday,

June 18th and the fact of my innocence will not have changed in the slightest.

Lights fade to dim then up on Julius.

JULIUS: (stands) Dear Manny, After reading the bald lie of the Justice Department that Mr. Bennett's visit was routine and that they initiated no deal was offered, I feel it my duty to present the facts as they took place last Tuesday Mr. Bennett opened the conversation and said:

MR. BENNETT: Mr. Brownell, the Attorney General, sent me to see you and he wants you to know that if you want to cooperate with the government you can do so through me. . . . If you, Julius, can convince the official that you have fully cooperated with the government, they have a basis to recommend clemency.

JULIUS: In the first place, we were innocent, that is the whole truth and therefore we know nothing.... You mean to tell me, Mr. Bennett, I said, that a great government like ours is coming to two insignificant people like us and saying, "cooperate or die"?

Lights fade on Julius and up on Ethel.

ETHEL: Dear Manny, This is to let you know my mother was here on Monday...

TESSIE: David seems to be holding up well.

ETHEL: Mother, whatever unfortunate fear of reprisal Davy might be harboring, it is my life that is in peril, not his...

TESSIE: I know, but he wasn't trying to . . .

ETHEL: . . . and further, if I, while awaiting electrocution, am not afraid to continue to assert my innocence and give the lie to his story, why couldn't he, in a far more advantageous position, be man enough to own up at long last, to this lie, and help to save my life, instead of letting it be forfeited to save his face!

TESSIE: So what would have been so terrible if you had backed up his story?

ETHEL: (beat, mouth opened in shock) What? And take the blame for a crime I never committed, and allow my name and my husband's and children's to be blackened to protect him? What, and go along with a story that I knew to be untrue, where it involved my husband and me?

TESSIE: Yes, you got me straight: I mean even if it was a lie, all right, so it was a lie, you should have said it was true anyway! You think that way you wouldn't have been sent here? No, if you had agreed that what Davy said was so, even if it wasn't, you wouldn't have got this!

ETHEL: (in protest) But, Ma, would you have had me willingly commit perjury?

TESSIE: You wouldn't be here!

Lights down on ETHEL up on DAVID.

DAVID: (addresses audience) They did not cooperate and clemency was denied.

NEWSIE 1: (appears) Spy Couple doomed to die!

Lights up on JULIUS in cell.

JULIUS: May 31, 1953, Ethel Darling, What does one write to his beloved when faced with the very grim reality that in eighteen days, on their 14th wedding anniversary, it is ordered that they be put to death? Beat, ETHEL and JULIUS walk out of their cells to the space in between. They stand together.

ETHEL: Dear Manny, The following letter is to be delivered to my children. Dearest Sweethearts, my most precious children, Only this morning it looked like we might be together again after all. Now that this cannot be, I want so much for you to know all that I have come to know. Unfortunately, I may write only a few simple words; the rest your own lives must teach you, even as mine taught me. At first, of course, you will grieve bitterly for us but you will not grieve alone. That is our consolation and it must eventually be yours. Eventually, too, you must come to believe that life is worth living. Be comforted that even now, with the end of ours slowly approaching, that we know this with a conviction that defeats the executioner!

JULIUS: Your lives must teach you, too, that good cannot really flourish in the midst of evil; that freedom and all the things that go to make up a truly satisfying and worthwhile life, must sometimes be purchased very dearly. Be comforted then that we were serene and understood with the deepest kind of understanding, that civilization had not as yet progressed to the point where life did not have to be lost for the sake of life; and that we were comforted in the sure knowledge that others would carry on after us.

ETHEL: We wish we might have had the tremendous joy and gratification of living our lives out with you ... Always remember that we were innocent and could not wrong our conscience. We press you close and kiss you with all our strength.

Next two lines said simultaneously.

JULIUS: Daddy

ETHEL: Mommy.

LIGHTS dim onstage as ETHEL and JULIUS turn and walk toward the judge's bench, they separate and walk offstage as DAVID speaks.

DAVID: (addresses audience) Two FBI men stood at a telephone line in the prison going to the U.S. Attorney General in Washington, D.C. They were waiting for last minute confessions as the Rosenbergs were taken to the electric chair.

NEWSIE 2: (appears) Rosenberg's die for spying!

REPORTER enters walks downstage center between the two cells.

REPORTER: (reporting) They died differently, gave off different sounds, different grotesque manners. Uh -- he died quickly, (electrocution of him begins, we hear the noise) there didn't seem to be too much life left in him when he entered behind the rabbi. He seemed to be walking in a cadence of steps of just keeping in time with the muttering of the Twenty-third Psalm.

As he dies, the same silhouette appears from the beginning of the show of JULIUS.

REPORTER: Never said a word. Never looked like he wanted to say a word. She died a lot harder.

Electrocution begins, ETHEL screams as monologue continues.

REPORTER: When it appeared that she had received enough electricity to kill an ordinary person and had received the exact amount that had killed her husband, the doctors went over to her and looked at each other rather dumbfounded and seemed surprised that she was not dead. And she was given more electricity which started again the kind of a ghastly plume of smoke that rose from her head.

Smoke billows on from offstage.

REPORTER: After two more little jolts, Ethel Rosenberg was dead.

Her silhouette appears as at the beginning of the show. Music begins to play as JULIUS and ETHEL move closer together to begin dancing with each other. Lights up on SAM and DAVID in same set up as show began.

SAM: So your testimony changed? You said your sister Ethel wasn't as involved than you said she was. David, who did the typing of the notes?

DAVID: I don't remember that at all. I frankly think my wife did the typing, but I don't remember.

SAM: You realize your testimony was what they built the
case against your sister on. Do you have any
regrets?

DAVID: I regret nothing

*LIGHTS fade out on DAVID and SAM. JULIUS and ETHEL
finish their dance, he dips her and pulls her up as they stare
lovingly in each other's eyes. FADE TO BLACK.*

END

Made in the USA
Monee, IL
06 February 2022